About the Book

You can't buck the establishment? You can't beat the system? You can't fight city hall?

WHO SAYS YOU CAN'T?

Ralph Nader took on the giant automotive industry in his battle for safer cars.

Gene Wirges exposed officeholders' shenanigans in his weekly *Democrat* and shook the powerful Arkansas political machine.

New Jersey's amateur conservationists didn't want a primeval swamp transformed into a jetport, and set out to save it in their own way.

Leon Sullivan used old weapons in new ways to win industrial opportunities for Philadelphia's Negroes— and economically deprived people everywhere.

Daniel Fader devised a way to educate the "uneducable."

Frances Kelsey and Helen Taussig protected thousands of American babies from hideous birth defects induced by a dangerous drug.

Joseph Papp wanted to give New York a free theater —and fought red tape, municipal antagonism and lack of funds to achieve it.

Who Says You Can't? is fast-paced, lively, thought-provoking reading. As Ralph Nader says: "It should be an inspiration to many young people who despair before they dare."

Who Says YOU CAN'T?

by

Beryl and Samuel Epstein

Coward-McCann, Inc.   New York

Third Impression

Library of Congress Catalog Card Number: 69-12661
Printed in the United States of America

CONTENTS

1. Lobbyist for the People
   Ralph Nader   9

2. Newspaperman vs. Political Machine
   Gene Wirges   41

3. Preservers of the Great Swamp
   New Jersey's Amateur Conservationists   88

4. Campaigner for Economic Equality
   Leon Sullivan   118

5. Crusader for Literacy
   Daniel Fader   154

6. Protectors of the Unborn
   Frances Kelsey & Helen Taussig   183

7. Protagonist of a Free Theater
   Joseph Papp   215

Who Says YOU CAN'T?

1

Lobbyist for the People

RALPH NADER

Ralph Nader, thirty-three-year-old Connecticut-born Washington lawyer, appeared on a 1968 *Newsweek* magazine cover as a knight in shining armor. The picture was produced by trick photography. The title beneath it—Consumer Crusader—had been bestowed on Nader many months before by the American public, as his legitimate due. He had become an authentic national hero when, after a battle involving a variety of cloak-and-dagger aspects, he triumphed over General Motors and the whole giant automobile industry.

Less than three years before that picture appeared Nader had been unknown beyond his own circle of friends, who were mostly other lawyers, newsmen and government aides. Then in November of that year he published a nation-shaking book called *Unsafe at Any Speed.* It was a slam-bang attack on American car manufacturers and the "safety establishment" which Nader claimed protected them from federal legislation.

It accused the car makers of subordinating human safety to auto styling, speed, power and "abject worship of that bitch-goddess, cost reduction." The book named names. It said, for example, that the 1960–1963 General Motors Corvair was "one of the greatest acts of industrial irresponsibility in the present century." It described accidents for which the car's instability had been responsible. It told of GM's successful avoidance of unfavorable publicity when victims of such accidents filed more than a hundred lawsuits against the company.

Unsafe at Any Speed declared that automotive engineers knew the dangers of the cars they designed. It blamed those men for failing to take a stand against the cost cutters and stylists who determined each year's new models.

The book also charged that the auto industry had long pursued a policy of blaming all auto accidents and injuries on poor driving, bad roads and traffic hazards—on anything but the vehicles involved. And the author stated that this policy had been consistently supported by the "safety establishment," the group of private and public agencies including some university research centers and the prestigious President's Committee for Traffic Safety, composed of private citizens and funded by the auto and insurance industries.

The book was, in effect, a vehement demand for federal auto safety legislation which alone, Nader believed, could protect the public. And it spelled out the various ways in which, up until then, the powerful auto industry had prevented its passage.

Science magazine reviewed the book a day or. so before its official appearance on November 30, 1965. "The companies, the researchers, the politicians and the bureaucrats will all find the book uncomfortable and will do their best to fight it down," the review said. "But it seems likely that the public will react differently."

The public did. The New York *Times* devoted a front page news story to the book on the day of its publication, and printed a review a few days later. The news story was a roundup of Nader's most striking charges. The review called the book "a ringing indictment of the industry . . . that, hopefully, will change Detroit's ways, voluntarily or otherwise." It added that the book "will not make pleasant reading in Detroit," but that "Mr. Nader's sobering pill is strongly recommended."

At least some people in Detroit were already reading it. On publication day a General Motors employee had telephoned Nader's publisher, Richard Grossman, and ordered 50 copies of the book. Aware that GM had no credit account with Grossman, the caller asked if the books could be sent at once and the bill for them paid later.

"Certainly," came the cheerful answer from the

publisher's office. "We're not worried about your company's credit rating. It's your cars we're worried about."

The next day, December 1, a New York *Times* headline said: CAR MAKERS DENY A LAG IN SAFETY. The manufacturers, according to the story that followed, had not attempted to refute any of Nader's specific charges. They did not even mention him by name. They simply denied all "charges that cars stressed power and styling at the expense of safety."

On the same day a spokesman for the American Automobile Association—one of the organizations listed by Nader as part of the "safety establishment"—said Nader's references to the AAA were "not only misleading, but untrue in many cases." But this spokesman also refrained from being specific. He quoted none of the individual references he was challenging.

A spokesman for the President's Committee on Traffic Safety said merely, not committing himself or his organization one way or the other, "If this fellow is right, people have been badly misled."

Soon a writer for *Life* magazine could tell his readers that "in Detroit, practically every auto executive has a copy of Ralph Nader's book on his desk. When they discuss it they can rarely avoid raising their voices."

In January 1966, when the book was less than six weeks old, two events of national importance occurred for which, many people declared, Nader and his book were largely responsible.

The President of the United States, in his annual message to Congress, called for federal auto safety legislation. He devoted only a single sentence to the subject. But that sentence caused more widespread discussion than any other part of Lyndon B. Johnson's address.

The second event was an announcement by Connecticut's Senator Abraham Ribicoff that a Senate subcommittee would hold hearings on the need for federal auto safety laws—and that Ralph Nader would be called upon to testify.

The industry's reaction to both these events bore out Nader's charges. "If Nader's book has infuriated Detroit [manufacturers]," *Life* reported, "the threat of federal legislation horrifies them."

In that same month of January Nader first began to suspect that he was being followed. At about the same time he received the first of a series of anonymous phone calls. "Cut it out now!" a voice sometimes said menacingly when Nader answered the phone. "Cut it out now!" Or a strange voice responded to his hello with "Why don't you go back to Connecticut, buddy boy?" Nader received six such calls on the night before he was to make his first appearance before the Ribicoff committee to present much the same charges he had made in *Unsafe at Any Speed*.

Other cloak-and-dagger business was occurring by then, too. Nader heard from various friends and acquaintances that inquiries were being made about him by professional detectives. His landlady told him that someone had called her to ask if Nader paid his bills on time. A stockbroker informed him of a visit from a detective inquiring about Nader's credit and his personal habits. One of Nader's former law professors at Harvard sent word that he had been visited by a man seeking information about Nader's private life for a client who, the questioner said, was considering hiring Nader. The editor of a law journal received a similar visit.

One of the most detailed reports that reached Nader came from his good friend, Frederick Hughes Condon, a Concord, New Hampshire, lawyer. Condon said he had been visited by a man who identified himself as a Mr. Gillen, and who explained that his purpose was to determine Nader's fitness for an important —though unspecified—position. But Gillen seemed chiefly interested in Nader's political beliefs and his personal habits. He asked if Nader owned a car. He wanted to know whether Nader, whose parents came from the Arabic-speaking land of Lebanon, was anti-Semitic. He asked about Nader's travels abroad. He asked why Nader, obviously able to support a wife, had never married.

To all these reports, and to the conviction that he was being "tailed" from place to place, Nader could add the experience of being accosted by two attractive young women, each of whom invited him to her apartment. One came up to him at a drugstore magazine rack and urged him to "join a foreign affairs discussion group," at her home that evening. The other sought him out, among other huskier male customers at a supermarket, and asked his help in moving a heavy piece of furniture into her flat.

By the end of February, Nader believed he had enough evidence to conclude that a determined effort was being made to discredit him and his testimony against the auto industry.

On Sunday, March 6, his suspicions—and the industry's reactions to them—made headlines across the country. The New York *Times* said:

CRITIC OF AUTO INDUSTRY'S STANDARDS SAYS
HE WAS TRAILED AND HARASSED:
CHARGES CALLED ABSURD

The story beneath the headline, written from Detroit by the well-known reporter, Walter Rugaber, began:

A leading independent critic of the auto industry has undergone an investigation of his affairs by private detectives.

The critic, Ralph Nader of Washington, has repeatedly charged that car manufacturers are guilty of unsafe design. His attacks have helped generate a controversy over auto safety.

The investigators, working for "unidentified clients," appear to have trailed Mr. Nader at different times in the last month and questioned a number of his friends.

Vincent Gillen of New York, an attorney and

detective, who said he had investigated Mr. Nader for an employment agency, said in a telephone interview: "I've had reason to believe from what we saw and what we heard that other people were investigating Nader."

He would not disclose the name of the employment agency.

Rugaber also interviewed unnamed industry leaders who all insisted that no auto maker was investigating Nader. One pointed out that little would be gained by such an investigation. Another said that anyone conducting an investigation of Nader would run the risk of being caught at it, and that no company would take such a risk. A third commented derisively on the clumsiness of the investigation as Nader described it. "You can bet," he said, "that if one of us was doing it, it would be a lot smoother. If we were checking up on Nader he'd never know about it."

Reaction from the Senate subcommittee was quick. Chairman Ribicoff, pointing out that intimidating or harassing a Congressional witness was a federal crime, asked the Justice Department to look into the matter. Senator Gaylord Nelson demanded a Congressional hearing.

On March 9 the front page of the New York *Times* erupted with a story that General Motors admitted it had conducted what it called a "routine investigation" of Ralph Nader. The GM spokesman declared the company was in no way trying to harass or intimidate the young lawyer. Instead, he said, it was merely trying to learn, through a reputable law firm, whether Nader was in any way connected with the lawsuits launched against General Motors by victims of accidents involving the GM Corvair.

Senator Ribicoff immediately announced that he was summoning General Motors executives before his committee to explain their actions. The Justice Department announced that it was starting its own investigation of the affair. Senators and Congressmen denounced the "snooping" in the press. Some called it scandalous.

On March 23 the nation's news media described in detail the next and climactic scene in the drama: James J. Roche, president of General Motors, the largest manufacturing company in the world, publicly apologized to the Senate and to the young lawyer who had dared to accuse GM of operating against the public interest.

Roche had opened his sensational statement by declaring that he had been as surprised as anyone when Nader first claimed that he was being investigated.

"Two days later," Roche continued, "in the process of ordering a formal statement denying our involvement, I discovered to my dismay that we were indeed involved. . . . This investigation was initiated, conducted and completed without my knowledge or consent, and without the knowledge or consent of any member of our governing committee. To say I wish I

had known about it earlier is an understatement. . . .
I deplore the kind of harassment to which Mr. Nader
has apparently been subjected. I am not here to excuse, condone or justify in any way our investigating
Mr. Nader. To the extent that General Motors bears
responsibility, I want to apologize here and now."

The General Motors president denied that his company was trying to intimidate Nader. He also denied
that the company had any responsibility for the harassing phone calls or for the attempts made by the two
young women to lure Nadar to their apartments.

At the close of Roche's statement members of the
Senate committee seemed convinced that he was personally blameless in the situation. But some committee
members were apparently not satisfied that GM had
been interested in Nader only for his possible connection with the Corvair lawsuits. Those Senators persistently questioned other GM officials, and were rough
in their treatment of Gillen, the detective who—a
reporter learned—had sent his field investigators a
memorandum which said: ". . . Our job is to check
[Nader's] life and current activities, to determine
'what makes him tick,' such as his real interest in
safety, his supporters, if any, his politics, his marital
status, his friends, his women, boys, etc., drinking,
dope, jobs—in fact all the facets of his life."

Gillen explained to the Senate committee that his
inquiries about Nader's sex life were prompted by the
fact that Nader was called a "woman-hater" in a high
school yearbook. Gillen also said that he had asked
questions about possible anti-Semitism on Nader's part

because some of Nader's relatives had been reported as having made anti-Semitic remarks. Following up such leads, Gillen said, had been done "in fairness to Ralph."

Committee member Robert F. Kennedy, angered at that testimony, snapped, "What the hell's this 'fairness to Ralph'? You have to keep running around the country proving he's not anti-Semitic or not queer? Ralph's doing all right."

"You and your family can be proud," Senator Ribicoff told Nader afterward, in an effort to make public amends for the harassment Nader had endured. "They put you through the mill and they didn't find a damn thing against you."

Nader subsequently filed suit jointly against General Motors and Gillen for invasion of privacy. He also sued Gillen alone, charging defamation. And Gillen, in answer, filed affidavits charging that GM executives had made false statements about the Nader investigation to Senator Ribicoff's committee. This prompted the Senator to ask the Justice Department to open an investigation to determine whether or not perjury had been committed.

Many months, even years, would pass before those cases would finally be settled. But other results of the whole affair came almost immediately because, as one Senator said, "Everybody was outraged that a great corporation was out to clobber a guy because he wrote critically about them. At that point everybody said, 'The hell with them.' "

While General Motors hastily called back 1.8 million Chevrolets, for correction of a throttle design defect from which GM was suddenly eager to protect the public, and while other car manuacturers followed suit by calling back hundreds of thousands of their own cars for replacements of "possibly" defective parts, Congress was debating and passing the kind of auto safety bill the industry had long dreaded.

It empowered the federal government, as Nader once put it, to require auto manufacturers to state, among other things, "such information as brake stopping distance, door strength resistance, tire handling performance and visibility levels in clear language according to common criteria."

It was not as good a bill as Nader had hoped for. Its passage did not mean that the federal government would necessarily make use of all the new powers granted to it under the bill, to control auto manufacture. But it did establish the principle that car manufacturers could be called on to meet federally imposed safety standards. It "set up a structure for progress," as Nader put it, toward what could become the nation's first effective auto safety program.

On September 9, 1966, President Johnson signed the bill into law. At the signing ceremony, according to the New York *Times,* "One of the last guests to file by the President and receive a handshake and a pen was Ralph Nader, crusading young author of the book, 'Unsafe at Any Speed,' which was instrumental in building public and Congressional support for strong auto legislation. The President shook Mr. Nader's hand briefly, without any sign of recognition."

Ralph Nader

Most Americans, by then, knew Nader by name if not by sight through the news media. The *New Yorker* magazine, taking its readers' knowledge of him for granted, published a cartoon in which a used-car salesman confides to a potential customer, "I happen to know Ralph Nader's mother drives this model." And all over the country reporters were busy trying to satisfy the public's sudden curiosity about this young man who had been ignored not long before, or scorned as "some kind of a nut," a Don Quixote tilting futilely at windmills.

If the reporters expected to discover a background of bitterness caused perhaps by a crippling auto accident in Nader's own youth, or the auto-caused death of someone close to him, they were disappointed. Nader had not been waging a vendetta against an enemy that had harmed him personally. He had been fighting a very different kind of fight.

Ralph Nader had begun his campaign for safer autos a decade before he wrote *Unsafe at Any Speed*. He had started along the road that would lead him to be known as the Consumer Crusader a good many years before that.

Born February 27, 1934, Ralph Nader grew up in his family's comfortable white clapboard house in Winsted, Connecticut. His father, Nathra Nader, who had come to the United States from Lebanon with his wife some years earlier, owned Winsted's Highland Arms, a popular bakery-restaurant.

Ralph was the last of four children—two boys and two girls. While his brothers and sisters were off about their own affairs, he was left very much to himself.

"I took walks in the woods," he has said. "I read a lot. I was a loner."

He is not regretting the fact. On the contrary he feels sorry, he says, for "young people who live regimented lives, who have no time to be alone."

Ralph had started school under what most people regarded as a handicap: he spoke Arabic more fluently than English. He had learned the language the year before when Mrs. Nader took her children to Lebanon for a nine-month visit with their sheep-farming grandfather and other Lebanese relatives. The Winsted school authorities had been reluctant to enter Ralph in the first grade when he returned. They suggested he remain in kindergarten until his English improved. Ralph's parents persuaded them to give the boy a chance. He finished the year as the best student in his first-grade class.

The members of the Yankee baseball team were Ralph's earliest heroes. He followed all their games, and tried to copy their exploits on the nearest vacant lot. Later he played basketball too. In high school, already towering toward his slim 6-foot-4-inch height, he might have become a valuable member of a school team. He wasn't interested. He wanted to enjoy sports, he explained once, not make them a regimented part of life.

By then Ralph was working after school and during his vacations in the Highland Arms. No one expected him to remain permanently in the family business.

All the Naders had taken for granted, from the time Ralph was a small boy, that he was headed for the law.

Years later, looking back on the time he spent as a waiter, Nader explained with a grin why he thought it had been valuable.

"A waiter has to adapt to all sorts of people and all sorts of situations," he pointed out. "And he has to do it publicly. He is always onstage. Even when he is mopping up the mess somebody's baby has made, he's performing for an audience. It's good experience for anyone who's going to be a lawyer."

The talk in the restaurant was good experience too. There was always a lot of it. One newspaperman recalls a Winsted resident saying about the place that anyone who went into it got "ten cents' worth of coffee and a dollar's worth of conversation."

Ralph's brother talked of the need to establish a community college. His father was vocal on a variety of town problems. And Nathra Nader had strong beliefs about his adopted county which Ralph says influenced his own early bent toward the law. Once, when reporters were questioning him about his suddenly famous son, Nathra Nader told them, "We made Ralph understand that working for justice is a safeguard of our democracy."

As a freshman at Princeton University Ralph immediately became aware of what he saw as opportunities to work for justice. He thought the school's curriculum was too rigid and should be revised. He thought expelled or suspended students should be given the right to appeal their expulsions. He thought the insecticide DDT was fatally injurious to birds and that its use on campus while students were walking to and from classes should be prohibited. (The dangers of DDT, widely accepted within a few years, were suspected by few people at that time.)

Ralph tried to win the support of other students for campaigns in support of his views. They responded with total indifference. He was amazed. He couldn't understand young men who seemed to accept all authority with sheeplike docility—even the unwritten law which declared that the only possible footgear for Princeton undergraduates was white buckskin shoes. Nadar wouldn't wear white buckskins—and the rest of the students were amazed at him.

He chose his major, oriental studies, partly because the curriculum offered more freedom than most, partly because it would give him the opportunity to learn more languages. "Languages are always useful," he says. By the time he was through school, and able to travel widely, he knew Spanish and Portuguese as well as Chinese and Russian and his half-remembered Arabic.

In the summer of 1955, between his graduation from Princeton as a Phi Beta Kappa and his entrance into Harvard Law School, Nader worked in a supermarket in Yosemite National Park. He drove there with a friend.

They argued good humoredly much of the way. Nader's friend, a fourth-year medical student, was determined to detour through as many national parks as possible. Nader wanted to visit every Indian reservation near their route. They managed to see a good many of both.

At Yosemite they had their first news of the devastating floods then sweeping the East Coast. Nader learned from front-page newspaper pictures that his father's restaurant had been totally destroyed. That fall, before he left for Harvard, he helped his father and brother dig out the seven feet of silt that had to be removed from the shattered structure before it could be rebuilt.

Ralph had been disappointed by Princeton. He was appalled by Harvard Law School. To his outraged eyes it seemed to produce lawyers equipped to serve only one kind of client—a big corporation or financial institution. Harvard Law School, Nader said once, was nothing more than a "high-priced tool factory."

The individual project he soon undertook there had nothing to do with either financial institutions or corporations. He wrote a lengthy paper he called "American Indians: People Without a Future." It appeared in April 1956 in the Harvard *Law Record,* of which he had become editorial manager.

His paper was headed by a quotation from a Crow Indian: "We are people who are better known for what we were than what we are, for what we are not than for what we are."

Nader's own first sentence was less dramatically impressive. "American historical and fictional writings have instilled in the American public a misinformed and highly inaccurate view of the American Indian."

But even though Nader was not yet a master of the hard-hitting phrases that pounded home his later attacks, he proved even in this first paper that he knew how to collect and marshal statistics. Comparing the health of Indians with that of the general population, he wrote: "Proportionally, the Indian population during 1953 had twenty times as many deaths from measles as did the non-Indian population, nine times as many deaths from tuberculosis, four times as many deaths from pneumonia and influenza and three times as many infant deaths."

He also proved that he had learned to use a great many sources other than the lawbooks attorneys customarily become familiar with. His figures on Indian health, for example, had been taken from the 1954 report of the Commissioner of Indian Affairs. He had also drawn from other government reports, from Acts of Congress, and from historical and anthropological writings.

Ralph Nader has been called a muckraker, a sensationalist who would rather expose unpleasant truths than tell pleasant ones. He says himself that he simply reports facts, and that he would lose his effectiveness if his opponents could ever convict him of inaccuracy. "I'm the one who can't afford to make mistakes," he said once. But even as a law student he was not afraid to expose his own attitudes to some of the facts he had unearthed.

Discussing the Navajos and those whites who had

imposed their own form of education upon them, for example, he wrote bitterly: "Rewarded as children in school for learning 'white ways,' as adults [the Navajos] are shunned for acquiring skills which make them competitors of their white neighbors. They are seldom received on terms of social equality and learn to expect employment inequality. Those same groups of whites who goaded them to give up 'ignorant Indian ways' now say: 'You can never trust those school boys. . . . Educated Indians are neither fish nor fowl. They give me the creeps.' "

After outlining the program which he believed the federal government should undertake for the betterment of Indians, Nader pointed out that in the past the government had rarely responded to any prods other than "votes, lobbies and other power factors"— none of which the Indians could bring forcibly to bear.

"Helping the Indian will not 'pay' in the sense that foreign aid 'pays,' " Nader concluded. "The impulse to better the Indian's livelihood can come only from a sense of our moral obligations and our humanitarian ideals."

Anyone seeking an explanation of Ralph Nader's crusading fervor needed to look no farther than that paper. His own humanitarian ideals and his strong sense of moral obligation had forced him to speak up for a people who, he felt, had no adequate spokesman. And his determination to make his voice effective had kept him at his long and diligent hours of persistent research.

The Indians of whom Nader wrote reprinted his paper in the Indian *Times,* with an editorial comment which began: "Several Indian people in the Denver Area consider this among the best information ever gathered, written, and published about American Indians in general. . . . On behalf of the officers and members of the White Buffalo Council of American Indians of Denver, and other Indian people, we express deep appreciation to Mr. Nader. . . ."

He was still in school when he first spoke up on behalf of the consumer on the subject of auto safety. In December of his senior year the Harvard *Law Record* published his "American Cars: Designed for Death."

Nader had never had an accident in his own car (which he gave up while he was at Harvard on the grounds that he didn't need it, though he kept his Connecticut license). He had been no more than shaken up a time or two in other drivers' cars. But he had seen a good many crashes and crash aftermaths on that drive to Yosemite and back. He had noticed great differences in the way cars and people survived collisions and other types of accidents. He had wondered what caused those differences. He had asked questions of such people as the Harvard Medical School doctors who saw many accident victims in the course of a year's work. And he had read and read and read.

The independent work that went into his paper had developed originally out of a student's routine exploration of the law's role in the aftermath of accidents. But what Nader wrote about was not how a lawyer could best bring suit for damages or defend such a suit. He wrote about a tragedy which lawyers seemed helpless to avert: the damage to human beings caused by defective or deficient auto design. He declared, in fact, that if victims of badly designed cars took their cases to court, they stood "a dim chance of success."

The paper was an astonishingly wide-ranging preview of *Unsafe at Any Speed*. Nader had already done much of the research that served as the foundation for that book, and reached many of the conclusions that he would express in it.

After discussing the statistics of highway deaths and injuries, and deploring the public apathy toward them, his paper referred briefly to the limited effects of driver education and highway safety law enforcement. They were, he pointed out, directed toward accident prevention rather than injury prevention. And it was injury prevention that he was already interested in.

He discussed what has come to be known as the second collision: "Most vehicular accidents can be considered as two separate collisions. First, the striking of the vehicle with another object and second, the striking by the occupant against the interior components of the vehicle (such as the steering wheel, dashboard, knobs, rearview mirror) or ejection through the door opened by impact.

"It is this second impact of the occupant against the inside of his car," the young law student wrote, "that does the killing and injuring, and there is nothing accidental about this."

One of the examples he gave to illustrate his point

had to do with "the apparently harmless glove compartment door."

"Under impact," he wrote, "those doors have been known to unlatch and drop down to become an unsheathed guillotine to decapitate a child or crush an adult's chest."

As he would do in his later book, he referred to the accumulated engineering know-how that could prevent many injuries. He mentioned a car developed by the Cornell Aeronautical Laboratory "with only a tiny fraction of the annual advertising budget of Buick," which embodied "over 60 new safety concepts which enable an occupant to withstand a head-on collision at 50 mph with, at most, only minor scratches."

And he accused the auto manufacturers of corporate irresponsibility, though not as vividly as he would do later: "Automobiles have been designed for style, cost performance, calculated obsolescence, but not in anticipation that they will be involved in a crash despite figures showing over 5,000,000 reported accidents yearly."

Nader also refuted—again, as he would do in the future—the manufacturers' claim that they built "what the consumer demands." That, he said, was not enough. "The average consumer is not in a position to know of the inter-relations between design and injury," he wrote. ". . . Even if he wishes to protest, how can he make it effective when one model is as unsafe as another and there are no alternatives open for selecting one manufacturer over another?"

New legislation to protect the consumer was needed Nader believed, and he cited precedence for it. "For example," he wrote, "meat must pass federal inspection before distribution; dangerous drugs cannot be dispensed without a licensed physician's prescription; airlines, railroads and other interstate carriers are required to meet safety standards regarding their equipment."

Nader had learned, and stated in his paper, that "for the past two years, a Special House Subcommittee on Traffic Safety has been conducting extensive hearings on automobile design." But he pointed out that the "sensational facts" which had come out of those hearings, though "perfect copy material," had been ignored by the press.

Nader's Harvard *Law Record* paper, so interesting today as a blueprint for his history-making book, was also ignored by the press when it appeared, as well as by the general public.

"Some lawyers read it," he once said, with a shrug. "But that was about all."

After finishing law school the following year, Nader did a six-month hitch in the Army and served for a time as a research assistant to Harold Berman, one of his former Harvard professors. Then in 1960, he joined a small law office in Hartford, Connecticut. His practice consisted of the young lawyer's usual assortment of cases in both criminal and civil law.

Recognition came to him briefly during those pre-Washington years through an article he co-authored for the *Reader's Digest*. Its subject was Roscoe Pound, long an outstanding member of the Harvard Law faculty. "The Grand Old Man of the Law," the article called him.

Pound was no longer active as a teacher when Nader met him, but was still vigorous as he approached his ninetieth birthday. He had, in fact, discouraged Nader's original plan of writing a full-length biography of him on the grounds that he meant to write it himself some day. Anecdotes about Pound were numerous. But Nader and Arthur Train, Jr., his co-author, ignored most of them to make one chief point: that Pound had never been satisfied merely to serve the law, but had always attempted to change it when he saw the need for a change.

"Throughout his life," the article said, "Pound has fought abuses in the law wherever he found them."

Nader had had no noticeable success at it so far, but he was still waging the battle he had begun at Harvard, the battle against what he regarded as abuses in the laws ignoring auto safety.

He had written an article for *The Nation* about that "safe car" designed by the Cornell Aeronautical Laboratory and Liberty Mutual Insurance Company, and mentioned in his Harvard *Law Record* paper. It was, his title claimed, "The Safe Car You Can't Buy" because automobile manufacturers refused to make it. The reason he quoted for their refusal was that the public was not interested in safety.

But *The Nation*'s circulation was small, and the

magazine was considered by many people as too "radical" to be taken seriously. So that article, and another that Nader wrote for the same publication, aroused little public interest and were ignored by the auto industry.

Nader tried other means of publicizing his one-man crusade. He talked about the need for auto safety legislation to any group that would listen. He testified in favor of it before committees of the Connecticut legislature and before similar committees in neighboring Massachusetts.

Most state lawmakers had been shying away from the whole subject for years, under pressure from the powerful auto industry which paid so many taxes, hired so many local constituents, and furnished such lavish entertainment to any legislator who showed the slightest curiosity about auto safety. Those elected officials did not want to hear the sort of thing Nader had come to tell them. One Massachusetts legislator clearly revealed his desire to be rid of Nader by his response to the young lawyer's statement that he lived in Connecticut. "Then what the hell are you doing in Massachusetts?" the man demanded.

Nader—who later quoted the automobile men's smug statement, "We know what the state tiger likes to eat"—grew more and more convinced that adequate safety standards would never be adopted on a state level. If they were ever to come into existence, he believed, they would have to be set by the federal government.

He was also becoming more and more dissatisfied in his role as a lawyer who spent much of his time trying to obtain compensation for clients injured in auto accidents.

He knew he was not, as a practicing lawyer, attacking what he regarded as the real problem.

"And it just didn't seem honest," he explained later, "to see the problem and not do anything about it."

In 1964 he abandoned his law practice to wage what he thought of as "total combat" against the auto industry on a national level.

He went to Washington and accepted a job offered to him through Daniel P. Moynihan, who had recently become Assistant Secretary of Labor. Moynihan too was concerned about auto safety. He had read Nader's articles on the subject. He wanted Nader to prepare a report outlining a federal auto safety program.

Ralph Nader worked on that report for a year. When it was finished he settled down to make available to the public the vast amount of material he had collected over the past eight years: he wrote *Unsafe at Any Speed*.

He submitted a detailed outline to one of the country's biggest publishers. It was refused with the explanation that the subject of safety had no popular appeal.

The smaller house of Grossman Publishers Inc. accepted the book that would so soon become a best seller in English and be translated into several foreign languages. Grossman prepared to publish the book in the late autumn of 1965.

In the meantime, during the spring and summer of that year, the climate for auto safety legislation changed rapidly. Ralph Nader had a vigorous hand in bringing about that change. He worked behind the scenes, as voluntary adviser and as originator of ideas and issues, for a Senate subcommittee investigating the adequacy of what states and auto manufacturers were then doing to promote highway safety. The subcommittee's chairman was Senator Abraham Ribicoff, former governor of Connecticut.

Nader's work with the committee made him, in effect, an unpaid lobbyist for auto safety on behalf of the consumer. As the consumer's spokesman, he was challenging the hugely powerful lobby of the auto industry.

Members of the Ribicoff subcommittee, using material provided by Nader, were soon mentioning specific auto manufacturers by name—an almost unheard-of practice before that time. Committee member Robert Kennedy, for example, publicized a Cornell University report which Nader thought should be brought to public attention. It included accident statistics which indicated that the door hinges of General Motors cars were more likely to fail than those of either Ford or Chrysler.

In the changing climate of that year other news also reached the public. A federal purchasing agency announced the list of 17 safety features it would like to see included in the thousands of cars it bought for government use each year. Senator Gaylord Nelson decided to offer a bill requiring those features in all cars starting with 1968 models. A group of doctors picketed the International Auto Show in New York, to dramatize what they had come to recognize as the industry's failure to build a safe car. The president of the American Trial Lawyers Association urged the federal government to do more to promote auto safety and said that his organization would start its own safety campaign in 1966. And when the industry continued to defend its own safety record, doctors and lawyers both protested that defense.

Damage suits for injuries attributed to poor car design were also winning wider attention. (A Detroit attorney announced that about one thousand such suits had already been brought against auto manufacturers for unsafe auto design and construction.) Nader had written in his book that a private lawsuit was "scarcely the best means for informing the public about a booby trap that suddenly leaves a two-ton automobile without brakes." But by the summer of 1965 reports of such suits were reaching a public newly educated to interpret their significance.

The Ribicoff subcommittee adjourned its hearings without recommending any federal policy changes. Instead it urged car manufacturers themselves to put more emphasis on safety in the future. But in October, New York's Governor Nelson A. Rockefeller warned that the federal government would indeed take over the control of auto safety if the states did not quickly assume responsibility for it.

And then, in November, Ralph Nader's book appeared and the drama rushed to its conclusion with the passage of the federal safety law.

Even before the law was signed Ralph Nader was being deluged with offers of lucrative jobs from industry and the legal profession. He accepted none of them. He felt his own crusade had just begun.

"He says he will make a career of opposing those centers of power—corporations, unions, government or whatever—he believes are infringing upon the public interest," wrote Patrick Anderson in "Ralph Nader, Crusader: Or, the Rise of a Self-Appointed Lobbyist," in the New York *Times Magazine.*

And so the pattern of Nader's life and his busy days did not change. He went on living in an $80-a-month furnished room and working out of a small cramped office. (Except for royalties from his book, and occasional lecture fees, he had no income.) He ate on the run. He still had no time for the game of basketball or chess he had once enjoyed. He still put in long hours reading through at high speed—and marking and clipping and sorting—the reports, periodicals, journals and letters which furnished him the ammunition he passed on to journalists and Congressional aides. He still ran up enormous phone bills checking and cross-checking every item for accuracy.

By 1967, while he continued to watch and criticize the administration of the auto safety bill, Nader was campaigning to win federal safety standards for gas pipelines, for the use of X-ray machines, and for the products of intrastate meat and poultry packagers and processors and commercial fishermen. And the public was following the progress of each of his new campaigns with fascinated attention. While he was waging a battle for new regulations to protect the consumers of meat, the *New Yorker* published its third cartoon about him. This one showed a roadside hamburger stand whose owner had erected a sign declaring proudly: RALPH NADER ATE HERE. Nader's campaign for stricter controls of the fish sold to consumers brought forth an editorial in *National Fisherman* which said: ". . . and now the Feds are sniffing down our necks—and they don't like what they smell. Auto industry Nemesis Nader is among the sniffers, and he's unhappy."

In the eyes of most people Nader was still the lone crusader—and he was a skillful enough lobbyist by then to know the public value of that image. But more satisfying to him than any individual law he had helped to get passed was the knowledge that he was no longer really alone. While he had influenced legislation he had also been influencing people.

"Ralph has pricked the conscience of many Congressional staff members," one of those staff members was quoted as saying. "It's very easy," he went on, "for Congressmen and their staffs to succumb to the Washington milieu. The industry lobbyists are chosen because they are charming and persuasive men. The Senator or Representative knows that consumer protection isn't good politics; the private interests are organized and the public interest isn't. It's easy to go along. What Ralph has done is force a lot of people to face facts, and to remember that they're here to represent the people."

Young law students and graduates all over the country were also writing Nader, offering to work with him —for nothing, if necessary. They were excited by what he had accomplished and what he still wanted to do. They identified their own goal of service to humanity with his. Instead of settling for jobs where they would work within the existing legal framework, they too wanted to fight abuses in the law.

"They could add a whole new dimension to the legal profession," Nader said of these young letter writers. "This opens up a whole new career pattern for them." And he began to think and plan toward a law firm whose sole client would be the public. It would be a firm staffed and equipped to carry on, on a larger and more effective scale, the work he was doing. He believed he could find financial support for such a firm through some private source or foundation, or eventually through the government, though it would always have to remain free to attack government bureaucracy if it was to do the work Nader envisioned for it. Ideally, he felt, such groups of professionals should be set up throughout the country. If consumers supported them by the payment of small annual dues, he has said, the consumers would be saved many times the amount it would cost them.

The questions Nader is asked, when he addresses a civic group or is interviewed over the air, reflect his widespread influence among people of all ages and varieties of background. The questions frequently suggest that people who want to do what he has done—who want to speak out against corporate abuses—do not know how to go about it. To Nader's puzzlement they seem to think he knows some trick, some arcane ceremony which they too should perform before daring to break their silence.

"They ask me, for example," he once said, " 'How should we go about starting a consumers' organization?' " He shook his head. He shrugged. He smiled. "I tell them, 'Start it. That's all. Just start it.' "

He was not saying that it would necessarily be easy for them to make their voices heard. He knew, better than most, what powerful pressures for silence might be imposed upon them. But he was saying that men *can* speak out, and that as more and more of them do so, they will bring closer that day when, as he once wrote, the world will "look back with shame on the time when common candor was considered courage."

His own common candor has proved what a single voice can accomplish. *Science* magazine, appraising his contribution to auto safety, might have been commenting on his continuing role as a consumer crusader when it said, "The answer to the perennial question, 'What can one man do?' seems to be that he can do quite a lot."

40

2

Newspaperman vs. Political Machine

GENE WIRGES

When Gene Wirges moved his family to Morrilton, Arkansas, in 1957, he wasn't planning to start a fight against a political machine—a fight that was to land him in jail, cost him his home and his business, and threaten his life. He and his wife Betty had chosen Morrilton because they thought it would be a good place to bring up their children, and because there Gene believed he could fulfill his newspaperman's dream of owning his own country weekly.

Gene Wirges—nobody calls him by his full name, Eugene—had investigated Morrilton (population 6,000, county seat of Conway County) before he and his wife decided to move there. They agreed that except for a few pleasantly shaded residential streets, it wasn't a pretty town. The tracks of the Missouri

Pacific Railroad ran through the middle of it, alongside its sun-baked main street, Broadway. The big red brick railroad station and a towering grain elevator near it dominated everything. Most of the business buildings were a squat two or three stories high, fronted by drab shop windows. Liquor stores were particularly numerous: Conway County was one of the few non-"dry" counties in that part of the state.

But Gene and Betty had found a house in the woods at the edge of town, where Betty could garden and the children could play. There was a good Catholic elementary school, and the promise of a Catholic high school by the time Ronald, their oldest, would be ready for it. Neighbors and townspeople seemed friendly; they had the old Arkansas habit of speaking a courteous greeting even to strangers in the street. And rimming the flat valley where Morrilton stood were the green hills of the Ozarks, which Gene and Betty both loved and wanted their children to learn to love too. Even after they had settled in Morrilton they were convinced, as parents, that they had made a wise choice.

And as a newspaperman Gene was sure they had also been wise to make a down payment on the Morrilton *Democrat* and its sister weekly, the Perry County *News*. At thirty he wasn't a novice at the business. He had already pulled one Arkansas newspaper out of the red, only to find that his businessmen partners, who had previously agreed to sell him their shares, were unwilling to do so once those shares became profitable.

Earlier Wirges had been a sports editor for two years on the *Evening Sun* of Jonesboro, Arkansas. And he had virtually grown up in the office of the state's leading newspaper, the Arkansas *Gazette* of Little Rock, where his father was an outstanding crime re-- porter and where Gene had worked himself up in six years from copy boy to general reporter and news photographer.

But Gene's faith in the future of his two new weeklies was based more on his knowledge of Conway County than on his own background. The county and Morrilton, its largest town, were, he believed, on the verge of a new prosperity. Lying along the state's chief economic axis, which runs through Little Rock to the east and on to Fort Smith on the west, Morrilton seemed a likely location for some of the new industry already springing up along that line. The number of tourists in the region, attracted by the Ozarks' recreational opportunities, was increasing each year. The county's agriculture, traditionally based on soybeans and cotton, also seemed to be headed in a new and more prosperous direction: Winthrop Rockefeller, one of the wealthiest men in America, had recently established a vast cattle-breeding ranch on the slopes of Jean Petit Mountain, a few miles outside of Morrilton. And there were plans under way to make the Arkansas River navigable, thus giving the region access to the whole water transportation network of the Mississippi and its larger tributaries.

"So we had a ten-year plan when we moved here,"

Gene remarked wryly more than a decade later, in 1968. "We were sure that within that time we'd have paid off our home and the newspapers too—that we'd be all set for the rest of our lives. That's how naïve we were!"

For the family's first three years in Morrilton the plan seemed to be working out. It was true that the town had not yet attracted the new industry Gene had anticipated, but he knew those things take time. His own business, however, was flourishing. He had bought new equipment that enabled him to print half a dozen papers besides his own, and to fill his steadily growing orders for commercial printing jobs. The originally small circulation of his papers was increasing. So was the amount of advertising they carried. Sheriff Marlin Hawkins, Conway County's chief law enforcer, tax collector, and most prominent political figure, had been friendly to the *Democrat,* and Gene had received a fair-share of the paid legal notices that are so important to the financial health of most weekly newspapers.

Occasionally a visitor to the little *Democrat* office beside the railroad tracks asked Gene if he planned to "do anything" about the Conway County political situation. Gene always shook his head.

"I wasn't editorializing about anything at all in those days," he said later. "I thought it would be preposterous for me, as a newcomer, to try to tell the people of the county how to run their lives."

Besides, the political situation was, so far as he knew, no different from that in any other Arkansas county. Of course all the officeholders were Democrats. There had been no viable Republican party in the state for years. This meant that any struggle for political power was within the Democratic party, and that the significant elections in Arkansas were the Democratic primaries. But since the people of Conway County had been electing Sheriff Hawkins to office regularly since 1950, their satisfaction with him seemed obvious. Certainly they swarmed around him whenever his big genial figure appeared in public, at a church bazaar or a cattle auction. And an entourage of admirers always trailed him on his morning walks from the courthouse to the coffee shop and back, and on his afternoon walks along the same route.

Then one day in 1960 a group of hill farmers from the north end of the county came into the *Democrat* office. They were tough men and they were angry. They told Gene they wanted his support for their plan to recall three members of their local school district board—to vote them out of office.

"You put in the paper that our kids take money to school for class rings—and then never get the rings," one of them said. "You write that they take money to school for class trips—and then never go on any trips. We say these three men are responsible for that. And we say we're going to get rid of them even if Sheriff Hawkins does back them all."

"I can't print charges like that just on your say-so," Gene told them. "But I'll make my own investigation. And I'll print the results of it—even if they're against you."

"They won't be," a farmer assured him.

Gene's investigation convinced him that the farmers had been telling the truth. He wrote an account of what he had learned.

"You'd better not print that!" a friend warned him. "The sheriff won't like it!"

"But it's true!" Gene Wirges said, and ran the story that same week on the *Democrat*'s front page.

With the *Democrat*'s backing the farmers won their demand for a recall vote.

"The two weeks that went by before that vote were wild," Gene recalled afterward. "Farmers driving along the back roads up in the hills were run off into the ditch. They got threatening phone calls."

When the polls closed, a group of vigilant farmers saw the regular election clerks begin to fill out a stack of unused ballots.

"What do you think you're doing?" an enraged farmer demanded.

"Just filling out the ballots for folks who weren't able to get out to the election," a clerk explained. "The way we always do, just to help out."

Instantly the farmer jumped onto the table and sat down on the ballot box. "You can fill those things out if you want to," he announced, "but you won't put any of them in this box!"

The clerks called for state troopers. The troopers arrived and ordered the farmer off the box. He refused to budge.

"Then we'll have to take you to jail," a trooper warned him.

"Then you'll have to find a cell with a wide door,"

46

the farmer retorted, "because this box is going right in there with me."

The troopers let him alone.

The time came to count the ballots. The farmers had previously told Gene there could be no more than 32 absentee ballots among them. But several times that number of sealed absentee ballot envelopes, each marked with a name, were dumped out on the counting table.

One farmer stabbed at an envelope with his cane and brushed it off onto the floor. "That woman moved out of the county thirty years ago," he said.

A clerk reached for the envelope. The heavy cane struck the floor within a hairsbreadth of his hand. The clerk left the envelope where it lay.

"And that man lives in another state and votes there," the farmer went on, and shoved another envelope to the floor.

When the farmer had finished looking over the envelopes, and thrusting to the floor those bearing the names of people he declared ineligible to vote, only some twenty absentee ballots were left.

The farmers won their recall by 17 votes.

They also elected all their own candidates in the special election called shortly afterward to fill the three vacant posts.

"They knew they could win that election, and they did! For once they had been lifted right out of the fear and hopelessness they had felt for years," Gene Wirges said, describing the event long afterward.

But at the time he had not yet begun to think of

Conway County as a place where fear and hopelessness were widespread. A primary election was approaching. He asked townspeople about the various candidates likely to offer themselves. His questions were pointedly ignored. People flatly refused to discuss the situation.

Curious, Wirges studied back records and discovered to his astonishment that there had been not one race for any political office in the area—city, county or state—since Marlin Hawkins had become sheriff. No candidates' petitions had been filed for the coming election either.

"Son," an old-timer explained to Wirges on the courthouse lawn, "we don't have elections here. We have see-lections. The Sheriff and his friends select the candidates. We just turn out and vote for 'em."

Now Wirges could understand the political gossip which had always declared that Sheriff Hawkins consistently delivered the Conway County vote to the administration of Governor Orval Faubus, who had by then been in office for several terms. It became clear to Wirges that the sheriff and his fellow county officials were not only an established local political hierarchy, but that they were part of the powerful and entrenched Democratic power structure of the state.

Even then Wirges did not intend to tackle the county political boss head on. But he did join other Morrilton citizens who had for some time believed that their town would grow faster—that it would actually attract some of the new industry it had been hoping for—if it replaced its mayor-and-council form of government with a city manager. A pollster brought in from Little Rock reported that 65 percent of Morrilton voters favored such a change. The proponents of the plan were confident they would win a referendum on the issue.

As the June 1961 referendum approached, Gene regularly exposed in the columns of the *Democrat* what he saw as the defects of Morrilton's mayor and city council. He repeated, for example, the often-voiced accusation that the municipal officials were responsible for the faulty planning of the city sewage disposal system. When the frequently flooded plant was again inundated during the May rains, Wirges left most of the upper half of the next *Democrat*'s front page blank. His caption beneath that expanse of white newsprint told his readers that he had hoped to reproduce a photograph of the flooded plant, but that he had not been allowed access to it to take the picture.

A week later the *Democrat* carried a front-page editorial headed WHY A CITY MANAGER? THE PEOPLE KNOW! In it he listed what he saw as the city's faults and its needs. One of those needs, he wrote, was "To be able to boast in fact that Morrilton is on the move (frontwards, that is)." Another he described as "To have our town known for its honest elections (honest, we mean it)."

By then everyone knew that Sheriff Hawkins was taking a hand in the municipal fight, and urging the defeat of the city manager plan. Hawkins had heard, rumor said, that a supporter of the plan had declared, "We're gonna clean up city hall first. Then we'll clean up the courthouse." Hawkins later explained his reaction to that statement to an out-of-state reporter. "At first I thought their motives was real good," he said. "They wanted to improve the city, and I felt there was room for improvement. But when they start talkin' out the courthouse, man, that's my bread and butter. It's my pro-fession. . . . I couldn't take that lyin' down. I'm a peace-lovin' man, but if a man wants to fight, well, I'll fight."

Even before this declaration of war, some local businessmen had begun to withdraw their ads from the *Democrat,* and subscribers had begun to cancel their subscriptions. Now there was an increase in this kind of economic pressure which, it seemed clear to Wirges, had been prompted by loyalty to or fear of the political machine.

His financial position was becoming shaky. Nevertheless on the night before the referendum he went to the expense of putting out his first extra. It carried a hopeful editorial urging people to vote. POLITICAL DOMINATION—IT'S NOT THE AMERICAN WAY, he headed it. That kind of domination, he wrote, imposed by the few on the many, was possible only when fear, apathy and ignorance paralyzed the voters.

On June 6, the day of the referendum, Morrilton was seething. Carloads of state troopers arrived early in the morning and took up stations around the town.

Tension built steadily during the forenoon. Many family men had sent their wives and children out of town, convinced that it was the only way to ensure their safety.

But as the afternoon wore on it became obvious that the vote would not even be close: the city manager plan was going down to defeat by a wide margin.

Slowly and dispiritedly the defenders of the plan drifted away from the *Democrat* office, where they had hopefully convened several hours earlier. When Gene Wirges walked over to the courthouse that evening, to watch the counting of the votes, he was alone. Inside the building he found himself in the midst of a boisterous crowd of Hawkins supporters, many of them already drunk in celebration of their assured victory.

Gene talked to the sheriff and the sheriff's two closest associates, a justice of the peace and a member of the County Election Commission. Voices rose. Soon he was arguing with the three men about the chances for a truly fair election in Conway County.

The rest of the room fell silent. The courthouse hangers-on listened in amazement to the tow-headed young editor. They had never before heard anyone actually argue with the officials who were so powerful in the life of the community. Slowly they closed in around Wirges.

Suddenly big "Bus" Hice, the county tax assessor, grabbed for Gene. Hawkins stepped between the two men.

Word of the near fracas got out. Hawkins supporters

gathered in a sullen crowd outside the courthouse. When Gene was ready to leave, a cordon of state police surrounded him and led him out of the building. Sheriff Hawkins walked beside him.

"He kept telling me," Gene remembered afterward, "that he couldn't guarantee my safety if I continued to write about politics. I said, 'Look at that mob there on your courthouse lawn. If ever there's a reason why somebody's got to write about politics, there it stands.' "

Gene's friends had hurried to the courthouse too, fearful for his safety. They picked him up in a car and drove him to his office. Closely following troopers guarded the street as long as Gene stayed there, and then trailed him to a friend's house and finally to his own home. It was after the troopers left, about 2:30 in the morning, that "some of the boys," as Gene put it, stoned his house.

"They didn't do any real damage," he said. "They just wanted to rattle—to make a big noise."

After that things happened quickly, and the pattern of charges and countercharges which soon developed became so complex that a full description of it would fill several volumes.

Within a few weeks after the referendum an election was scheduled, to name a replacement for a recently deceased member of the state legislature. Hawkins's "selection" for the post was Loid Sadler, county election commissioner and one of the sheriff's closest associates. But this time the regular party nominee faced an opponent. Backed by the *Democrat,* and assured of support by many people, young Houston Mallett, a feed dealer, had agreed to run for the office.

The campaign was lively. Again there was hope among the forces for better government, as they had come to think of themselves.

But Mallett was badly defeated. In Catholic Point, his own district, he received just 2 votes to Sadler's 93.

Afterward a puzzled Mallett told Wirges that five of his Catholic Point friends swore that they had voted for him.

"Five!" Wirges repeated, and decided to look into the matter.

He talked to those five persons, and then to others whose names they gave him. Soon he had found fourteen Catholic Point voters willing to sign statements that they had cast their ballots for Mallett. Wirges had also learned of nearly fifty other persons who, though unwilling to sign statements, privately assured him they had voted the same way.

"One house I visited I remember particularly," Wirges recalled later. "Three people lived there. When I told them why I had called, and about some of the signed statements I had, they looked at each other sheepishly. Then they told me that before the election they had all agreed to vote for Mallett—and that they had been suspicious of each other ever since the 93–2 vote was announced. They had all been wondering which of them had gone back on his word. They were really glad to see me—glad to know they didn't have to go on distrusting each other.

"But I wasn't so welcome at other places," Wirges added. "A lot of people just wanted me to get out. They were afraid to talk."

Before he could write an account of what he had learned, Wirges received a phone call. "If you think Catholic Point was bad," the caller said, "you should come to Austin."

Wirges did. There he found that the number of votes cast was actually greater than the number of qualified voters in the district—a claim he would be unable to substantiate because some of the voters lists had "disappeared." (His efforts to find those lists went on futilely for months. The lists were still missing years later.)

During Wirges's visit to Austin, a shot rang out and a bullet struck a tree trunk a few feet above his head.

"Of course I couldn't prove it was meant for me," he said afterward. "It could have been a stray bullet from a hunter's gun somewhere outside of town— though the hunting season hadn't yet opened at the time."

That summer of 1961 Gene had serious financial problems. Because of his decreased income he had fallen behind in the payment of his state employment security taxes. An understanding tax office representative had helped him arrange to pay off the sum in installments. But as Gene was getting ready to go to press with his Catholic Point and Austin election stories, a deputy sheriff affixed a notice to the *Democrat* office door. The notice said the newspaper would

Gene Wirges

be sold to satisfy a claim for delinquent employment security taxes.

Shocked and incredulous, Wirges called the man he had dealt with in the tax office only a few days before. The man was equally shocked. He declared he knew nothing of the posted notice. The main agency office in Little Rock, however, admitted to Gene that it had approved the posting of the sale notice at the request of Sheriff Hawkins.

Gene managed to pay off the full $600 immediately. The notice came down from the door. And the *Democrat* of July 20, 1961, made exciting reading in Conway County. The sudden surge in newsstand sales that week indicated that even people who had canceled their subscriptions wanted to see what the *Democrat* had to say.

The chief headline, over the story of the Catholic Point and Austin voting, read:

EVIDENCE OF VOTING IRREGULARITIES REVEALED
BY CITIZENS SEEKING BETTER GOVERNMENT

The lower part of the front page was devoted to a story which Gene explained he had written earlier and had been reluctant to print, but was printing now because of his recent experience with local pressure politics. It was an account of the election night when Wirges had been threatened by "Bus" Hice and when his home had been stoned.

The paper also carried an angry editorial headed THE TRUTH ABOUT PRESSURE POLITICS, relating the story

55

of the sales notice that had appeared on his door, and its reason for being there.

A week after that paper appeared, Wirges was making his usual Friday afternoon rounds along Morrilton's Moose Street when big "Bus" Hice came up to him and knocked him down. It was a heavy blow. Hice weighed 220 pounds to Gene's 155. And Hice struck him again before Gene could get to his feet.

"If you ever print anything about me in that paper again," Hice said, "I'll whup ya every time I see ya."

Gene's face and one leg were cut and bruised. The doctor who X-rayed his head said he had suffered a concussion.

Gene accused his assailant of assault and battery. Hice was duly fined in the amount of $32.85. Gene then filed a damage suit against the sheriff's friend for $30,500, and the case finally came to trial the following spring.

"The courtroom howled," Gene said, describing the event, "and Hice himself was barely able to keep a straight face as he told his story. His evidence was that I'd come up to him, said 'Hi, Bus, looks like you Communists won again'—and then hit him."

Even the judge smiled openly at the word picture of slight Gene Wirges attacking the burly Hice.

The jury retired briefly and announced itself divided, 6 to 6. The judge declared a mistrial.

Gene was convinced that any future effort to bring his suit into court would end the same way. He had learned that "Bus" Hice could indeed "whup" him whenever he liked, without ever suffering any stiffer penalty than a light fine.

Gene had been unable to drive a car for weeks after Hice's assault. Betty, expecting their fifth child, drove him on his rounds and shared his worries over the economic crisis that grew more serious every day.

Advertisers who had continued to patronize the *Democrat* until now suddenly stopped buying space in the paper. The reasons they gave were varied, but to Gene their underlying motive was clear—fear of angering the political overlords. Commercial printing orders fell off sharply too. And from the diminishing number of legal notices the *Democrat* received from the state, county and federal governments, Gene knew that this important source of revenue would soon dry up completely.

Suppliers from whom Gene bought his paper and equipment began to call him to say they had heard rumors that Sheriff Hawkins might have to close the *Democrat,* and that therefore they could extend it no further credit. They asked Gene to settle his accounts with them in full, immediately.

Even the *Democrat*'s stringers, the housewives paid by the line for the social notes they brought to Gene each week, came tearfully to the office to explain that they had been threatened with the loss of their husbands' jobs if they continued to work for the *Democrat.*

Gene's friends, now banded together in a Better Government League, were feeling the pressure too. They lost business. One was warned that his adopted children might be taken away from him. A doctor was being driven to the decision to close his clinic and move away. "I didn't want to spend the rest of my productive life in a county like that," he was later quoted as saying.

It was at about this time, too, that young Ronald came home from school one day bruised and bloodied. He had never been in a fight before. His mother was angry with him. "But you should have heard what they were saying about Dad!" Ronald protested.

"That is no excuse!" Betty Wirges told him. "Your father has done nothing to be ashamed of. He has never told a lie and he has never knowingly hurt anyone. So you don't have to fight for him. He doesn't need protection."

But she and Gene both admitted their relief when, shortly afterward, Ronald suddenly shot up to a height of over six feet, and the boys who had been taunting him just as suddenly fell cautiously silent.

The outside world's first recognition of the struggle taking place in Conway County came when Gene was still subbornly trying to obtain a grand jury investigation of the vote frauds he had uncovered at Catholic Point and Austin—and being awakened at night over and over again by anonymous threatening phone calls. In September 1961, *Time* magazine carried a story which said that for Gene Wirges running the *Democrat* had been a "basic course in the varieties of violence." It described the assaults that had been made upon him and his property, and the political machine he was attacking. *Time* called it "an entrenched and well-oiled apparatus" run by "Marlin Hawkins, 47, a paunchy, cigar-chomping native son. . . . Although the county government has yet to take any action," the story said, after explaining Gene's editorial stand claiming vote frauds, and, it added, although the city manager scheme Gene had backed had been badly defeated, "there are increasing signs that Wirges's fearless leadership has pierced the public apathy that has helped keep the county machine in power.

"Said Gene Wirges last week, blooded but unbowed," *Time* reported, " 'I think they're on the run.' "

The story made the sheriff angry. He gave up cigars and began to chew gum instead. But if Gene himself had any idea that the sheriff's political machine would shrivel in the spotlight of national publicity, he soon learned otherwise. And his own quoted remark, about his adversaries being "on the run," would also soon appear to him as evidence of naïveté not yet outgrown.

In October a grand jury was finally convened to look into his vote fraud charges. It was the first grand jury assembled in Conway County in twelve years, a fact that seemed to imply either that the residents were remarkably free of wrongdoing, or that there was an equally remarkable lack of curiosity about their behavior on the part of the county's law enforcement agencies.

Gene immediately objected to the jury on the grounds that all its members were adherents of what he now openly called the Machine. The judge waved away the objection, assuring Gene that the jurymen would "do a good job."

Gene, though doubtful now of the outcome, turned over to the jury the list of election irregularities he had compiled—there were more than 80 instances—together with a list of the citizens who could testify to them. Among the documents he submitted were statements from several persons who declared they had looked through the window of a polling place and seen election officials placing ballots in the ballot box after the polls were officially closed.

The jury's reaction was to berate those witnesses for not having stepped in and made citizen arrests if they had actually seen ballot stuffing. It hinted to them that they might be charged as accessories for not having attempted to stop what they said they had seen. Then the jury decided that the alleged ballot-box stuffing could not possibly have been seen at all, because of the screen over the window through which it had allegedly been witnessed.

Gene responded to that with the kind of journalism *Democrat* readers were growing accustomed to. He stationed a friend inside the polling place, holding a watch in his hand, and photographed the man through the window. The resulting picture, reproduced in the *Democrat,* proved that through that window it was even possible to read the time on the face of a watch.

In its official report the jury admitted that there had been "irregularities" in the election vote tallying. But it went on to exonerate the officials involved. Either they had been ignorant of the election law, the jury said ("Officials? Ignorant of the law?" Wirges demanded) and therefore had not willfully violated it; or the violations could be overlooked because they were, as the jury put it, "customary and had been carried on during many previous elections."

Wirges published the jury's decision, convinced that his readers could judge for themselves the quality of men who regarded voting irregularities as excusable, provided they were repeated often enough to become "customary."

In the same issue he dramatized the fact that the Better Government League had not yet succeeded in its attempts to inspect the presumably public voting lists that would back up Gene's claim of irregularities in the election that defeated Houston Mallett. He headlined his boxed story

90 DAYS AND
STILL MISSING

"On June 6, 1944, Allied forces invaded the beaches at Normandy, France," the story read, "and began their slow and bloody path toward central France.

"This great campaign of World War II required only 81 days.

"For 93 days the Better Government League has been attempting to obtain the official voting lists from 10 missing Conway County ballot boxes, but the attempt at liberation of these public records has been fruitless.

"Which only goes to prove," the story concluded,

"that some wars are more easily fought than others."

Before the week was out Gene received a letter from the grand jury foreman hinting that Wirges himself might land in jail if he continued on the path he had chosen. Gene published the letter too.

In the spring of 1962 the *Democrat* backed the Better Government Organization's full slate of candidates for county officials in the Democratic primary: sheriff, judge, and some twenty lesser posts.

"By then the whole county was divided," Gene remembers. "You were either for us or against us."

Enough people proved to be in favor of the Better Government group to elect three of its candidates. But even this meager success turned sour. One of the newly elected men "joined the enemy," as Wirges put it, the morning after election. A second moved away before taking office. The third, J. G. Boudra, was refused a seat at the first official meeting he tried to attend, on the grounds that his claim to be a Democrat was false—that he was in reality a Republican. Boudra promptly filed suit to obtain his seat, and won. His fellow committee members then voted whether to seat him or not, and voted no. Again Boudra filed a suit, and again he won. By then a year had passed since his election, but at last his right to take his seat on the Democratic Central Committee was assured—or so he believed and so the *Democrat* reported. What actually happened was that the committe simply did not meet again until Boudra's term of office was over.

"That kind of stalling technique," Gene Wirges

once said, "frustrated dozens of taxpayers' suits, brought with the help of the Better Government group, against various kinds of political fraud. Orders to call up the suits were simply ignored. Nothing happened. They were just allowed to lapse."

In the meantime Gene's debts were piling up. And suddenly he faced financial ruin from an unexpected quarter. He had some time earlier made a down payment on another weekly newspaper, the *Bulletin* of nearby Jacksonville, then decided the purchase had been unwise and had sold the paper to a third party who agreed to assume Gene's regular payments to the original owner. But the third party had been unable to meet those payments, and they had fallen back on Wirges. And the holder of the mortgage suddenly demanded the full sum still owing to him: $11,399.90.

Gene was unable to pay that amount immediately. A judgment was issued against him. Once more the sheriff posted a Notice of Public Sale on the door of the *Democrat*. The paper was to be sold at public auction at eight o'clock on the morning of July 5, 1962.

With the help of friends, and because the mortgage holder had said he was in desperate need of cash, Gene quickly offered him a sizable sum. The offer was flatly refused. Gene understood the reason for that refusal only later, when he learned that the judgment had been taken over by one of Sheriff Hawkins's political allies, who had thus become Gene's creditor.

On the evening of July 4, only hours before the sale was scheduled to take place, a Perry County doctor,

Stanley G. Gutowski, whom Wirges had never met, delivered to Gene's attorney a certified check for $11,399.90. He was opposed to boss rule, the doctor said, and for that reason wished to purchase the judgment so that the *Democrat* need not be silenced. He made it clear that he would hold the mortgage until Gene could conveniently pay it off, however long that might take.

Before Gene could report the news to his friends, a group of them called on him with a paper sack full of money. They had collected it, they explained, to stave off the sale. "After all, it's *our* paper," they said. Gene explained to them that their generous gift was no longer needed.

At seven o'clock the next morning out-of-town newsmen were gathered in front of Gene's office waiting to report the demise of the battling *Democrat*. TV cameras were trained on the office door, still bearing the Notice of Public Sale. Gene telephoned Sheriff Hawkins and told him the judgment had been paid.

Hawkins tried to seize Dr. Gutowski's check and apply it to some of Gene's other debts, so that the judgment would remain unpaid. Gene's lawyer blocked that move. Then Hawkins demanded a sheriff's fee of $500 for holding the sale.

"But the sale's not going to take place," Gene pointed out.

Hawkins replied that having made arrangements for a sale, he expected his fee in any case.

Aware that the *Democrat* could be sold to meet this

64

new demand, Wirges told the sheriff he would have his fee as soon as the bank opened, and waited at the bank until its door was unlocked.

A few minutes later he handed Sheriff Hawkins $500, with the public statement that he was doing so under protest. The suit he immediately filed to reclaim the fee was one of those that was "just handed around" and which, years later, had still not come to trial.

Once more the *Democrat* had been saved. That night, when a Morrilton attorney telephoned Wirges and offered him $50,000—collected, he said, from a number of his clients—if Gene would leave Conway County and "never even drive through it again," Gene laughed and hung up.

One week later the paper was again in danger of being sold. On this occasion the announced sale was to meet a demand of the Internal Revenue Service for the immediate payment of $7,000 in federal tax arrears.

Again help came in the nick of time, and from a new source. Winthrop Rockefeller, who had already given Morrilton an elementary school and a community service building, unexpectedly set up an escrow fund equal to the amount of Gene's unpaid taxes. The money would remain in the account, Rockefeller said, and would be available for payment of those taxes in the event that Wirges was unable to pay them himself.

Rockefeller's explanation of his action was, Gene's

supporters agreed, an example of masterful understatement. "It seemed to me," Rockefeller said, "there were political pressures being put on him that stifled freedom of the press."

Wirges used to the full the chance he had thus been given to continue his fight. He had been backing an antimachine slate of candidates in the 1962 elections which were then about to take place. At least one of those candidates, for a school district director's post, was considered to have an excellent chance. And when the "live" ballots were counted on election night he was ahead 200–132.

Hawkins's election officials, seemingly unperturbed by this tally, then counted the absentee ballots. There were 152 of them, and only nine were marked for the man Wirges had backed. He lost the election, 209 votes to 284.

Wirges and an attorney hired by a newly invigorated Republican State Executive Committee investigated those absentee ballots. They learned that 66 of them should have been declared invalid and omitted from the count, because they were unsupported by written applications from the voters named on them. The two men also discovered that about ninety of the voters who had used absentee ballots were present in the voting district on election day, and could have—even may have—voted in person. The Republican-hired attorney immediately prepared lawsuits to challenge the election. Gene spread the story over the front page of the *Democrat,* and wrote a scathing editorial comment on it in his regular column, "Around the Hub."

Gene was discovering other Conway County voting irregularities too. With Republican help from the Midwest, for example, he learned that three of the county's absentee voters were simultaneously casting ballots in Michigan. Since Arkansas law prohibited double voting, Gene presented his evidence to the county's prosecuting attorney. No action was taken. And when Gene offered proof of the double voting to the Department of Justice, in Washington, it disclaimed jurisdiction. Regulation of voting, the Department spokesman said, was in the hands of the state—even if the votes concerned were cast in a federal election.

Wirges then turned to an investigation of county funds. He discovered, for example, that Judge Tom Scott, the county's chief executive, had not once during his term of office submitted the annual statement of county finances required from his office. Wirges also learned that Scott's court had heavily overspent its 1962 funds, without explanation, and that the county had spent more than $24,000 for "paupers and welfare" over a three-year period, while its more populous neighbor, Pope County, had spent less than $6,000 during this same time.

Wirges published all the information he uncovered in the *Democrat*, and publicly demanded an explanation for it. None was forthcoming. Persistently he continued to ask questions of the political machine, on these and other matters. One subject he often angrily discussed editorially was Morrilton's lack of growth, which he openly blamed on the machine.

When he reported that one corporation had by-passed Morrilton as a plant site because of the "political situation" there, he asked his readers to speculate on how many other new sources of jobs and incomes had been lost to the community for the same reason.

When he reported that Conway County had become notorious as a "speed trap," and that motorists were going out of their way to avoid driving through it, he asked Morrilton residents to calculate the loss in business revenue that this policy of Hawkins's machine was costing them.

Wirges also attacked the county politicians for the bad condition of Conway's roads and bridges. An unpaid columnist for the paper, whose colloquial style amused many readers, often added her voice to that charge. "Well, another week and they still ain't scraped our roads," she wrote in one column. "These roads look like we're getting ready to fight a war and they already got the foxholes dug."

The columnist, Mrs. Eulena Stout from the small community of Birdtown, had told Gene that she did not want her name to appear in the paper. Wirges had therefore protected her anonymity by heading her column "Birdtown Birdie Sez." There was frequent speculation as to the columnist's identity. Wirges himself was often suspected of being "Birdie," especially after the column began referring regularly to "His

Majesty," whom everyone understood to be Judge Scott, and to "the King," who was equally widely recognized as Sheriff Hawkins.

In the summer of 1963 Gene Wirges was honored with the Elijah Lovejoy Award for "courage in journalism." That same summer he was sued for libel, in the amount of $100,000, by the county clerk, C. C. Brewer. Brewer claimed he had been libeled in Wirges's articles about the school district election, articles in which Wirges had pointed out irregularities in the handling of 152 absentee ballots. Brewer did not accuse Wirges of lying. "The fact that he published it is the thing I'm complaining about," Brewer said.

The *Democrat* was hit by a second libel suit two months later. Its complainant was County Judge Tom Scott, who said his reputation had been damaged by various statements in the Birdtown Birdie column.

Brewer's case was presented by Nathan Gordon, best-known lawyer in the county and at that time lieutenant governor of the state.

"The blackest day ever in Conway County history was the day Gene Wirges arrived," Gordon told the jurors. He reminded them that "under Babylonian law, a person who committed libel was put to death. Later, in Great Britain under King Alfred, the penalty was cutting out the offender's tongue. I think sometimes that this is a pretty good remedy for such an offense," he said.

Brewer's name had never been mentioned in the

articles he was complaining about. His case therefore depended almost entirely on one basic point: that even though he had not been named, his reputation had been hurt because everyone knew that he handled absentee ballots.

Wirges's lawyer, Tom Eisele, asked each juror if he did in fact know who handled those ballots. All claimed they did not. It was therefore obvious, Eisele said, that so far as the jurors were concerned, Brewer's reputation could not have been damaged by the *Democrat* articles since they could not have connected them with him.

The jurors disagreed. In less than an hour they awarded Brewer $50,000 for the loss he had suffered through the articles, and another $25,000 in punitive damages—an extra punishment for Wirges.

A few days later the second libel suit against Wirges and the *Democrat* came to trial. Again the lawyer for the plaintiff was Nathan Gordon. Again the jurors made no secret of their friendliness of his cause. The jury foreman, in fact, was one of Gordon's business partners.

Gordon accused Wirges of libeling Judge Scott in the "Birdtown Birdie Sez" column with a statement that "the King shakes your hand with one hand and picks your pocket with the other."

Wirges testified that the epithet "the King" was never used to refer to Judge Scott, but to Sheriff Hawkins, and he produced many Birdtown Birdie columns to prove it. Therefore, he claimed, Scott had not been libeled. Wirges further claimed that the comment was not libelous in any case because it referred to a politician's official rather than personal conduct, and that any public figure's official conduct was subject to public criticism. And, finally, Wirges testified that he had not written the column in question. When asked the identity of the author, however, he refused to divulge Mrs. Stout's name.

Once again the jury needed only an hour to find Gene Wirges guilty. This time the penalty was $200,000, and the judge sentenced Wirges in addition to ten days in jail for contempt of court, for refusing to name the author of "Birdtown Birdie Sez."

Wirges appealed both libel verdicts and the contempt of court sentence. But before the appeals could be adjudicated, Scott and Brewer moved to take over the *Democrat* in payment of their claims. A scant hour before their representative appeared at the newspaper office, one of Gene's friendly creditors, a Little Rock businessman, turned up with a court order permitting him to take over the paper to satisfy his own claim against the *Democrat*.

For still another time the *Democrat* had been kept out of the hands of its enemies, but those enemies had now won a partial victory. The paper's new owner, unwilling to subject himself to libel suits, refused to keep Gene on as the *Democrat* editor. The new editor he hired to replace Wirges was instructed to run a noncontroversial paper, and obeyed orders.

In the meantime, shortly before Christmas 1963,

Gene was broke and out of a job. He was about to lose the home he and Betty had chosen so happily five years before. His children received Christmas gifts that year only because Gene's lawyers bought them. Loyal Morrilton friends collected a small sum of money to help keep the Wirges family going.

"His crusade was over," a Little Rock newspaperman wrote sympathetically of Gene Wirges, in an article which appeared some months later in the *Atlantic Monthly* magazine, under the title, "How to Lynch a Newspaper."

The sympathetic author was mistaken, however. Still "blooded but unbowed," as *Time* had described him more than two years earlier, Gene Wirges was using his unsought leisure to search for an answer to a question that had troubled him for some time: Why did Conway County audits show so little money collected in traffic fines, when its law enforcement officers made about five times as many arrests as were made in nearby counties?

"It didn't make sense to me," Wirges recalled later. "The number of arrests in a single year might be somewhere around 2,000. And I'd heard of sizable fines being paid—fines of 70 or 80 dollars or more. But all the money collected in fines for that year, according to the county audit, might be as little as $5,000."

Records turned over to him by a disgruntled state employee, who hoped Wirges would "get" something on the machine, corroborated Gene's own idea of the size of the fines paid. The records were of the arrests made over a period of six years by one state police officer; they showed that many of the fines he had collected were indeed large—so large that the small totals shown in the county audits could be explained in only one way, in Wirges's opinion: a great deal of money simply disappeared, after the fines were collected but before they were recorded in the county books.

How that disappearance was managed, and where the money went, Wirges did not know. But he had his suspicions, and he thought he could verify them if he dug further.

He discussed the problem with Winthrop Rockefeller, who had already begun to involve himself deeply in Arkansas politics.

"I told him," Wirges recounted afterward, "that we'd got hold of some interesting records. I said we couldn't be sure what we'd find if we kept looking, but that we thought it was worthwhile to go ahead. He agreed to help pay our expenses. And that's when our investigation really started."

Gene had already been promised the help of several friends. He divided them into teams and supplied each team with a camera. Then he made certain that no whisper of what he was after leaked out.

"I wouldn't have been surprised," he has said, "if the records we wanted to photograph had disappeared as mysteriously as those voting lists that have never turned up, once word got out that we were interested in them. Of course they're public records, and no one had the right to prevent us photographing them—but those voting lists are supposed to be public records, too."

First Wirges and his photographic teams, using the magician's device of misdirection, asked for the police records of truck-weight violations and other documents which could offer no threat to officeholders and which the authorities, though reluctant to open their files at all, permitted them to see. Underling clerks soon became accustomed to seeing the teams at their monotonous and obviously harmless task, accustomed to bringing out the records they asked for. And those same clerks responded automatically to the requests Gene and his friends finally made to them one day. Before the clerks realized what was happening, Wirges and his friends had photographed the arrest and charge records they wanted.

Each of the dozens of case records, of which Wirges now had photographs, demonstrated the pattern he had suspected. One case, for example, was that of a man involved in a minor accident on a highway near Morrilton. Arrested on the spot by a state policeman, he was charged with driving while intoxicated—in police parlance, charged with a DWI. According to the policeman's record of the arrest, the man paid $80.35 in fines and costs. But the country records of the same arrest—same date, same name, same identifying numbers—duly signed by a Conway County justice of the peace, showed that the man had been charged with disturbing the peace and speeding, and that he had paid only $14.00 in fines and costs.

No record existed anywhere of the missing $66.35. So far as Gene Wirges could determine, it had reached the sheriff's office and then vanished.

To clinch his case, Gene and his wife Betty then traveled hundreds of miles through half a dozen states, seeking out the persons named on the records they had accumulated.

Some of the people they found were eager to help them, but could offer no evidence beyond an uncertain recollection. Others were unwilling to talk to them at all. One minister, determined that his congregation should never know he had been accused, however unjustly, of driving while intoxicated, refused to admit he had even been in Conway County on the day a man with his name and his car and license number had been arrested there. But many people were eager to help and could do so. They agreed to have their statements tape-recorded. They signed affidavits. They produced canceled checks showing the actual amount of the fines they had paid, and permitted Wirges to photograph them.

By the end of six months Wirges was satisfied that his case was unassailable. He was further convinced of it when Sheriff Hawkins's supporters came forward with the suggestion that Gene and the sheriff forget past differences and "pull together" in the future. Gene made it clear that his plans for the future did not include that kind of cooperation.

By then a group of Gene's friends had bought the *Democrat* so that their common purpose would once again have public expression. They did not name him editor, because they believed the position would simply involve him in further legal harassment and physical assault. Instead they named Betty as the *Democrat's* editor and Gene went to work as her assistant.

"They won't strike her," Gene once explained, grinning at Betty across their small office. "They don't like what she does. But here in Arkansas even the toughest men have a code of chivalry when it comes to actually attacking a woman."

Betty had never had any desire to run a newspaper, but she accepted her new job as part of the life she had come to accept.

"It takes getting used to," she admitted once, and described the difficulty she and Gene had had when they tried to rent a house to replace the one they had lost. Door after door had been slammed in their faces. They finally found a temporary haven only when one owner told them firmly, "All right. I'm going to rent to you and that's that. I don't care what they say."

Gene Wirges began the new phase of his campaign against Sheriff Hawkins and the machine by taking the evidence he had collected to the prosecuting attorney. He was told that it involved events so far in the past— Gene had investigated records for the years 1954 to 1962—that investigation of them was prevented by the statute of limitations.

Gene called a press conference. Reporters from all over the state, and from news services as well, who had been watching his career with interest, turned out to listen to his tape recordings, look at his photographs, and hear his conclusions about the disappearance of certain sums of money.

Sheriff Hawkins immediately demanded a grand jury investigation to exonerate him of any wrongdoing. The jury was summoned. Willingly Wirges appeared before it as the first witness, and handed over his records. The result was an indictment of Wirges for slandering Hawkins. And when Wirges refused to answer further questions until the members of the jury studied the records he had submitted to them, he was cited for contempt of court and locked up in the evil-smelling county jail. He remained there for four days, having been denied any opportunity to change his clothes, brush his teeth or even wash during that whole time.

When he was released he was charged with conspiracy, and Winthrop Rockefeller's name was brought into the case by the judge.

"The harm this great crusade of Mr. Wirges and his financier friend has brought to Conway County can never be measured in dollars and cents . . ." the judge told the jurors. "We are actually living in a state of anarchy. Do you want to continue to live in chaos, or should we find out who the culprits are and handle them in accordance with the law?"

The jurors answered his question to the judge's satisfaction. They declared the Wirges evidence against Hawkins to be false and unsubstantiated, "and further, that the statute of limitations on said allegations, if true, had long since run . . ." They found Wirges guilty, fined him $250, and sentenced him to a four-month term in prison which—as had now become a habit—Wirges appealed.

Once more a national magazine, this time the *Saturday Evening Post,* ran a story on the man it called "The Embattled Crusader of Conway County." It declared that "after years of attacking the local political machine, a fighting editor is headed for jail."

During that October 1964 trial, Winthrop Rockefeller was running for governor of Arkansas on the Republican ticket. There was nationwide curiosity about the campaign of a man who had once been widely known as the playboy of the Rockefeller family, and his new interest in politics raised some skeptical eyebrows.

But the New York *Times,* among other influential publications, took him seriously. "In his campaign," the *Times* reported, "Mr. Rockefeller has sharply attacked the power that county judges and sheriffs wield in Arkansas."

And the *Times* continued, in words that would have had special interest for any Morrilton reader, "Observers believe he has sought to use Conway County as an example of what he contends is the sort of power that can be built up by functionaries under the one-party political system Arkansas has had for a century."

Though Rockefeller lost the election, he garnered

a respectable number of votes. His announcement that he intended to run again in 1966 was heartening to Wirges and others who had been fighting the battle of Conway County.

There was other good news for Wirges too, at about the same time. A few months after the 1964 elections —and not unconnected with Rockefeller's good showing in it, in the eyes of many Conway County residents —three of Gene's appeals reached the higher courts of the state, and three of the charges against him melted away. The most recent—the conspiracy conviction— was reversed because the indictment was declared to be "fatally defective." The two judgments against him in favor of Brewer and Scott were set aside. The Brewer conviction was specifically described by the Arkansas Supreme Court as an act of "community prejudice."

"I thought the tide was beginning to turn," Wirges remembered afterward. And he added, perhaps forgetting that he had spoken the same words five years before, "I thought we had them on the run."

"They" had not, he soon realized, run very far. In October 1965, Wirges was reindicted for slander and conspiracy against Sheriff Hawkins, and also indicted on a surprising new charge, perjury. He was accused of having lied during the Scott libel trial when he denied having written the Birdtown Birdie column on which the libel charge was based.

Among the jurors selected for the new trial, over the objections of Wirges's lawyer, were some who had served on the 1964 jury which had twice indicted Wirges on charges that were later thrown out. Now these jurors assured Wirges's lawyer that this time Wirges would indeed get a fair hearing, although one admitted under cross-examination that "everybody has their minds made up." Again Nathan Gordon was present, now as a "volunteer" assistant to the prosecuting attorney.

The chief witness against Wirges was the woman whose anonymity he had protected during the Scott libel trial. Now Mrs. Stout was testifying against him. She claimed that although she had written most of the Birdtown columns, Gene Wirges sometimes added paragraphs of his own to what she had brought him. He had, she swore, added the one about "the King." Even when Wirges produced from his files columns in her own handwriting which she claimed he had written, she stuck to her story. She explained that she often copied columns after they were printed, for use in a book she planned to write. She had kept those handwritten copies in a box in her house, she said, but could not produce them because they had recently disappeared—stolen, she clearly implied, by Gene Wirges.

As in every perjury trial, the basic question was the credibility of the two chief witnesses: Whose word was more to be trusted, that of Mrs. Stout or Gene Wirges?

In an effort to cast doubt on the credibility of Mrs. Stout, who claimed that she had been married four times and that her only brush with the police had come over a traffic ticket, Gene's lawyer had the woman's past investigated. He discovered that Lena, as she was known, had been married eleven times. ("From the best I can figure out," Mrs. Stout said later, "when things would get dull, I'd go and get married again so there would be something to celebrate. The guys that I was married to—I don't even remember their names. I started drinking. I guess I was one of the worst alcoholics that ever was.") Gene's lawyer also learned that Mrs. Stout had been arrested in four states for a total of at least 22 times, for drunkenness, vagrancy, prostitution and other offenses.

In a résumé of this and other cases in which he had been involved, which Gene Wirges wrote for the *Democrat* some time later, he described the introduction of some of this evidence (the jury was not permitted to hear all of it) in a characteristically colorful style: "Now it was beginning to appear as if Lena wouldn't know the truth if it wrapped around her like a python. . . . At about this juncture of the trial, Nathan Gordon was making less noise than a butterfly with a sore foot landing on a marshmallow."

But the prosecuting attorney assured the jurors that Lena Stout was a woman of integrity, and urged them to bring Gene Wirges, perjurer, to justice.

It was almost two o'clock in the morning when the jurors left the courtroom. They returned just before 4 A.M. with a unanimous decision: Wirges was guilty.

Two days later the sentence was handed down: three years at hard labor in the State Penitentiary. Wirges posted a $5,000 bond and—automatically—appealed.

A year and a half later the *Democrat*'s front page

carried the 8-column headline, SUPREME COURT CLEARS WIRGES, and an editorial that began: "Conway County —already the butt of every judicial joke in the country —received another swift boot to its posterior this week as the Arkansas Supreme Court tossed out the ridiculous three-year perjury sentence against former *Democrat* editor Gene Wirges."

A full page of that same issue was devoted to reprinting the many headlines used in the newspaper over the years for stories about Gene Wirges's indictments, trials, and convictions. ("He has been indicted more times than he can even remember," the *Saturday Evening Post* writer had said of Wirges.) Some of the indictments had never resulted in a trial. None had survived appeals to higher courts.

A few months later, in December 1967, a suit in which Gene Wirges was not a defendant came to trial. This was a taxpayers' suit against Sheriff Marlin Hawkins to compel him to account for the money he had collected in traffic fines. The suit had been originally filed in May 1965, by thirteen of Wirges's friends, some of whom had helped him gather the mass of evidence they would present—the photographed arrest records, taped interviews, signed statements and canceled checks.

Once again Conway County was making nationwide headlines. SHERIFF ON TRIAL ACCUSED OF FRAUD was the New York *Times* headline over its story of the opening of the case.

"Sheriff Marlin Hawkins is on trial here accused by a group of taxpayers of defrauding the county of some

$160,000 in traffic fines," the story began, and went on to summarize Wirges's battles with Conway County politicians, his defeats in the lower courts and his vindication by the higher tribunals of Arkansas. Then it said:

> The taxpayers' attorneys . . . contended that Sheriff Hawkins had failed to account for $240,-640.84 in receipts from traffic arrests in Conway County. Making allowances for fees that the sheriff could have paid to deputy prosecuting attorneys and justices of the peace, Mr. Hawkins still must account for $162,640.84 he collected between 1954 and 1966, they said. . . .
>
> The main witness was former state trooper W. O. Jack Stone, who testified that he saw Mr. Hawkins and a justice of the peace changing the records on traffic fines two or three times while he was assigned to the county. He said one would read names out of receipt books and the other would enter the names in the justice of the peace transcript books with lesser charges and smaller fines.

The *Times* also reported that when one of the taxpayers' attorneys said that nearly all of the sheriff's receipt books were "mysteriously missing," Hawkins admitted it, but that "his attorneys produced a few loose receipts subsequently. . . ."

The case dragged on. There were rebuttals and rebuttals to the rebuttals. The sheriff testified that some of the discrepancies charged against him could be explained by the fact that sometimes, after having received a bond from someone who had been arrested, he later returned the bond money on the "oral order" of the justice of the peace. The fact that such an order was not written down, he said, was the reason there was no record of where the money had gone.

The sheriff also testified that he sometimes returned a motorist's bond, and then later paid the motorist's fine himself, out of kindness—and that the county actually owed him money.

"Are you telling this court," Hawkins was asked once by a taxpayers' lawyer, "that you refunded Mr. Berry's bond money, the $200, and then a few weeks later in your settlement, paid the $170 to the county yourself?"

"I imagine I did," the sheriff replied. He spoke "weakly," the *Democrat* noted, in its account of that day's court session.

At the end of seven months the judge ordered Hawkins to pay the county treasury just $10,082.20, and Hawkins declared the size of the judgment proved he had won a "moral victory." Dissatisfied taxpayers insisted the Hawkins case was far from over, and began to plan their next move.

Life went on pretty much as usual for the Wirges family during the long-drawn-out trial and its aftermath. There was the Wednesday evening, for example, when Gene was called upon by Jerry Bennett, a convicted felon, who had been willing to testify that Gene tried to bribe him. Bennett didn't like what Gene had printed in the paper about him—a reproduction of the district attorney's accusation against Bennett, later upheld by a conviction. Bennett arrived at the Wirges house with the loud announcement that he had come to beat Gene up.

It was the dinner hour. All five Wirges children were at home. With them was a young boy who went to high school with Ronald and his sister, Vicky. They could all hear the conversation that took place at the door. Betty Wirges stood beside her husband.

"Why don't you just go home?" Wirges said to the visitor. "You know I didn't offer you any bribe. Gordon knows I didn't. And he knew I'd find out the truth about you and print it. Don't you understand that? He and Hawkins are too smart to use physical violence on me themselves," he went on patiently, "but they don't mind if some of you boys try it—and get into trouble as a result. They think you're expendable. Don't you realize that? I have nothing to discuss with you until you're ready to tell the truth."

"I have no use or respect for anyone who lies," Betty Wirges put in, "and I know that's what you did when you claimed my husband offered you a bribe."

"How do you know I'm lying?" Bennett demanded.

"Because I know my husband—and that's more than your wife could say," Betty told him.

Finally Bennett turned away. "Well, just don't you ever put anything in your paper about me again—or I really will beat the hell out of you!" he threatened over his shoulder.

"Look in next week's *Democrat*," Wirges advised him.

Betty was ashamed of what she had said. "That

wasn't very nice of me," she insisted, when her grinning husband repeated her words to friends. But Gene was pleased with the remark, and used it in the front-page story he wrote describing Bennett's menacing call.

The Wirges children had taken it all in stride. But their visiting friend had found it pretty exciting, 19-year-old Ronald said. "He's never been around here before when one of these things happened," Ronald explained.

That same day the *Democrat* had printed one of its frequent roundups of the situation.

"The questions are obvious," the concluding paragraphs began.

"Who's leading whom?

"Where is the community going?

"Why has the community strangled while neighboring towns have progressed by amazing leaps and bounds?

"How could it happen?

"When will people get enough?

"Well, we have to believe the questions DO have answers. And we happen to believe it doesn't have to be this way. It will take a little courage, and a little honesty, and a lot of common sense. 1968 could be the year. It must be."

That very morning Gene had said to visitors who had arrived to hear the Wirges story, "You know, we didn't mean to get committed to this thing. But that's what we are—committed. And when we look back on it all now, we know we'd do the same thing again if we had the chance. After all, if a newspaper can't tell the truth, then what's a newspaper for?"

Betty Wirges nodded her agreement. She would be glad if the fight could be over. She even thought she could see a glimpse of the end of it. "When Sheriff Hawkins appears in public now," she said, "—and it doesn't happen every day, the way it used to—there's no longer a crowd around him. Usually there's only one man, or perhaps two. And when he drops in on some local event, like a club picnic, people turn away from him, as if they realize that he's on his way out. They're deserting, really. Sometimes I feel almost sorry for him."

"Oh, Mom!" Ronald said.

"No, I mean it," Betty told him.

Both Betty and Gene Wirges knew by then that the defeat of one political machine could not guarantee just and honest government for Conway County forever. They knew that if their battle did end, they might have to start another one some day—and perhaps another one after that. They knew the commitment they had made might require them to spend their lives on a battlefront.

But they were willing to do so, if it was necessary. They both still agreed with what Gene had often said: "We feel this community—where our children are growing up—is worth it."

3

Preservers of the Great Swamp

NEW JERSEY'S AMATEUR CONSERVATIONISTS

Ten or twelve thousand years ago, give or take a few thousand years, a glacier retreated slowly northward across New Jersey. It left behind a lake some thirty miles long and ten miles wide. This prehistoric body of water, named Lake Passaic by geologists, found a path to the sea by a channel that is now the Passaic River. The lake has long since vanished—it took about a thousand years to drain—but it left behind in its turn a vast wetland area. Part of this area, situated in what is now Morris County, N. J., is the 7,000-acre Great Swamp, a scant thirty miles from the heart of New York City.

In 1959, after centuries of placid existence, this tract of marsh, meadow and low woodland became a bone of contention, a prize in the battle between a powerful government agency and a group of determined citizens. That year the Port of New York Authority announced that the Great Swamp could be ditched, drained and filled to form the site of a new metropolitan jetport. Almost overnight the normally calm population of Morris County went into a roiling boil. Soon the entire state was involved. The Great Swamp became the subject of private and public argument as pro- and anti-jetport partisans girded for the fight.

Long before European settlers came to the New World, American Indians had fished and tracked game in the Great Swamp. Evidence exists that prehistoric hunters roamed the region about nine thousand years ago. Early New Jersey colonists cut firewood in the swamp's more accessible woodlands. Charcoal made from swamp hardwood was used to smelt iron for Revolutionary War armament. The swamp's higher and drier areas were hayfields and pastures until a few decades ago, when residential communities replaced farms in this now heavily populated part of New Jersey.

Despite man's long use of the swamp, nothing had ever really threatened its existence before 1959. Even when land values boomed under the relentless post-World War II demand for more housing, realtors left the swamp's vast acreage alone. The task of draining and filling the swamp—even its higher areas are too wet for good building practice—seemed too tremendous a project for even the most ambitious land developer. Generally speaking there was not what could be called an active market for Great Swamp acreage.

The only recent demand for it had come from local conservationists deeply appreciative of the swamp's unspoiled wilderness and unhampered wildlife. One conservationist organization had acquired about 450 swamp acres, and was planning the gradual accumulation of more. Other organizations also hoped eventually to buy some of the Great Swamp and set acreage aside as bird and animal sanctuaries. But there was no great urgency about any of these projects. Except for drivers using the few paved roads across the swamp, almost no one entered it from one year's end to the next except bird watchers, amateur botanists and biologists, and teachers from nearby schools and colleges who used the swamp as a living laboratory and outdoor classroom. So the news that the Port of New York Authority was casting covetous eyes on the swamp's 7,000 acres came as a sudden and stunning shock to everyone in the area.

The Port Authority is an awesome adversary. Not only does it have vast sums at its command—it was planning to build a $200,000,000 jetport—it also has the power of eminent domain. It can take land, paying a fair price for it, whether or not the owner wants to sell. Even the land already bought by conservationists could be acquired by the Port Authority if it so chose.

Very soon after the announcement of the proposed jetport, the forces for and against it were aligned. A number of businessmen, construction workers, realtors and others who foresaw benefits from a Morris County jetport were quick to applaud the Port Authority's interest in the swamp. They urged local and state government agencies and officials to do everything possible to persuade the Authority to proceed with its plans.

Arrayed against this pro-jetport coalition were those who visualized the construction of a noisy jetport in their midst as sheer calamity. These were, for the most part, people who valued that part of New Jersey as a quiet place in which to live. They included a large segment of the population.

A rallying point for the anti-jetport citizenry was the quickly formed Jersey Jetport Site Association. With a sizable budget, and a staff of public relations experts, this group mounted a massive campaign aimed at convincing every nearby resident that a jetport would mean the virtual end of their middle- and upper-class residential communities. In the newspapers, over the airwaves, and at numerous public meetings, Morris County homeowners were bombarded with dire predictions of what would happen to their neighborhoods if the thunder of jet planes sounded regularly overhead.

Just as vociferous, however, were the claims made by the jetport proponents. Building trades labor unions pictured the benefits to the workingman of a multimillion-dollar construction project. Business groups argued that a jetport would bring new prosperity to the region, and that the thousands of jetport employees coming into Morris County would need housing and shopping facilities which would further stimulate the economy.

Inevitably the debate grew acrimonious. Inevitably,

too, it began to take on political overtones as proponents and opponents tried to convince the state's
elected officials to support their own point of view.
When Governor Robert Meyner voiced support for
the jetport, he became the subject of bitter denuncia-
tion and was publicly suspected of devious political or
personal motives.

One segment of the anti-jetport group was composed primarily of the conservationists who had long
had a special feeling for the swamp. They too hated
the changes a jetport would make in their environment. They hated even more the thought of losing
the Great Swamp as an irreplaceable home of plant
and animal life, as a wilderness of peaceful solitude.
They too were willing to fight for the swamp, but
they wanted to do it in their own way. So when the
Jersey Jetport Site Association was formed, to wage
its no-holds-barred war against anyone who favored
the jetport, a group of conservationists decided to
form a committee of their own.

These men and women—there were fewer than a
dozen of them—met for the first time late in December
1959. They were active members of various nature
groups, garden clubs and civic associations. In one
way or another they had been striving for years to
maintain the natural beauty of their part of New Jersey. They had fought the haphazard spread of housing
developments. They had opposed wholesale conversion
of fields and woods into immense shopping centers.
They had urged elected officials—often successfully—to

provide funds for parks and recreation areas. They had championed legislation to end stream and river pollution. They had counseled against the indiscriminate use of those chemical insecticides that are as lethal to wildlife as to insects. They were, in essence, shining examples of the public spirited citizen, the promoter of idealistic schemes to benefit the community.

The nucleus of the group was its three co-chairmen, Mrs. James W. Hand, Mrs. Robert L. Lloyd and Dr. Robert Krebs, and its executive secretary, Mrs. Arthur G. Fenske. Also active were John T. Neal Jr., of the New Jersey Audubon Society, Fred Sacksteder of the Summit Nature Club, and M. Hartley Dodge, a wealthy retired business executive who had previously donated land for a Morris County Park and long demonstrated in many other ways his deep interest in preserving the area's rural aspects.

Together with the other committee members they decided to undertake an enormous task: to buy the Great Swamp, or at least enough of it to leave a balance too small for a jetport, and then deed their land to some organization that would preserve it as it was.

Out of the committee's first exploratory meetings came the conviction that the Great Swamp would be safest from man's depredations if it were turned over to an agency of the federal government. This would remove it—though the committee members did not plan to make an issue of this themselves—from the political fighting over the jetport already going on in New Jersey. And, since the Department of the Interior is the nation's principal guardian of natural resources, the group decided to offer the swamp—if and when it could be bought—to that Department for use as a National Wildlife Refuge.

Committee members were therefore soon conferring with representatives of the Fish and Wildlife Service of the Interior Department.

From them they learned that any area the Service would agree to accept would have to be large enough to be managed effectively. This meant it would have to include enough land to allow for the creation of ponds for nesting and migratory wildfowl, without flooding adjacent land that might be privately owned; adequate acreage for the planting of grain to attract and feed wildfowl; and sufficiently large and suitable areas to permit the laying out of trails and the construction of administration buildings. A Great Swamp National Wildlife Refuge, in other words, would have to consist of several thousand acres.

Fortunately this disturbing news was not the whole story.

The committee members also learned that the Fish and Wildlife Service had long been interested in the most watery portions of the Great Swamp—areas referred to in the Service as "prime wetlands"—for their value to migratory birds. The Service was, in fact, empowered to purchase such prime wetlands on its own, provided they were of sufficient size to meet government-imposed standards. It had been prevented from even considering the purchase of Great Swamp wetlands, however, because each was far too small to meet those standards, and because they were separated from each other by low meadows and hillocky woodlands, varieties of terrain for which the Service was not permitted to spend its limited funds.

To the committee members from Morris County the solution seemed obvious: they would purchase and turn over to the Service all those areas the Service itself could not buy.

The government representatives agreed to the plan, but with obvious reservations. They were clearly doubtful of the committee's ability to fulfill its self-appointed task. The amount of land the committee would have to purchase, to make possible an eventual Wildlife Refuge, added up to 3,000 acres. The cost of that much land would be approximately three-quarters of a million dollars. And at least a considerable portion of that vast sum would have to be raised quickly, before the Port Authority could take steps to acquire the Great Swamp for its own use.

But the committee members themselves were confident. They were practical enough to recognize their lack of experience for such a job. But they knew they had energy and conviction, and they were unafraid of setting out on a learn-as-you-do basis, since no instruction book was available on how to raise hundreds of thousands of dollars to buy a swamp. With little else except three slide projectors donated by Dodge, and the use of Mrs. Fenske's kitchen as their headquarters, the amateur defenders of the Great Swamp went to work.

Fortunately they were able to affiliate almost immediately with the North American Wildlife Association, of which Dodge was a trustee. This prestigious organization has a roster of distinguished trustees and officers in every part of the country. Its history in the field of conservation is widely known and respected. Contributions to it are exempt from federal taxation.

As the Great Swamp Committee of the North American Wildlife Association, therefore, the little Morris County group found itself the instant beneficiary of the Foundation's prestige and—perhaps even more importantly—of its tax-exempt status, often a vital consideration to potential donors with large incomes and large income taxes.

Beginning early in 1960 Mrs. Fenske's kitchen became in turn a map room, a planning center, a meeting place and a mail room. Most frequently it was a mail room because communication was the committee's basic tool for arousing public support of its cause. A constant stream of circulars and letters began to flow out of the impromptu headquarters. Some described the swamp's abundant bird population. Some were devoted to the variety of wild plants that grew there. Others spoke of the animals, aquatic and terrestrial, that found homes in the secluded swamp depths.

The committee also sent out letters to garden clubs and other nature-minded groups, offering to present slide-illustrated lectures on the Great Swamp. Since speakers for club meetings are often hard to come by, these offers were eagerly accepted. A pair of committee members was assigned to fulfill each obligation. One member operated the slide projector; the other gave a running commentary on the pictures being shown. Mrs. Fenske, with no more training for such performances than the ordinary housewife, took a course in public speaking in a determined effort to do as good a job as possible. The purpose of the lectures, of course, as of the letters and circulars, was the stimulation of contributions to the swamp fund.

The committee sent out news releases about its activities, and most of the local papers printed them. Morris County editors and readers alike seemed intrigued by the handful of Great Swamp defenders who were tackling such an enormous project. Almost from its inception the group received large amounts of neighborly praise for its efforts and its aim. But cold cash was not forthcoming at anywhere near the same rate.

"We were all novices," Mrs. Fenske has said. "We simply didn't know how to ask for money."

There were other things the committee workers didn't know how to do. For one, they seemed unable to write a news release that would be accepted and used by the Associated Press or any other nationwide news service. This meant their work was not becoming known outside their own communities, although they felt sure it would arouse interest in the crowded cities nearby, if the residents of those cities could only hear about it. Surely, the committee members told each other, a New Yorker would want to preserve a wilderness so close to his own doorstep that he could visit it in an afternoon; he would want it kept for his children and his children's children, so that they could learn what the world had been like before man covered so much of it with his steel, concrete and asphalt. But somehow the committee members could not get their message into the papers and onto the airwaves that brought the city dweller his news.

One day, after brooding over their failure in this respect, Mrs. Fenske drove to the nearest office of the Associated Press. Her youngest child was with her, because she couldn't afford a baby-sitter. Her purpose was to deliver her latest release and to ask what had happened to all those she had previously sent there.

The busy AP office manager answered her question by pointing to his wastebasket, and then went on with his work. Mrs. Fenske realized that the new release in her hand was undoubtedly headed for the wastebasket too.

"But why?" she asked, and stood her ground until the editor looked up again.

She did not leave his office until her persistent questions had elicited a short but intensive lecture on the art of writing a news release so attention-catching that it was bound to be sent out over the AP news wire.

Thereafter the news bulletins that issued from the Fenske kitchen were considerably more professional in style. They landed in city newspapers, and sometimes in papers far from New Jersey. And they brought forth at least a small stream of donations from people who had never before heard of New Jersey's ancient swamp, but who wanted to help save it as a matter of principle.

Few donations, from near sources or far, were larger than ten dollars. Most were smaller. Each was gratefully received and dutifully acknowledged. But the meager sums, and the mounting costs of mailings, kept the committee members on a constant search for ways to carry on their work with as little expense as possible. When they needed new color slides for their talks, for example, they didn't even consider hiring a photographer. Instead they got in touch with local photography clubs.

"Photograph wild life in the Great Swamp!" they suggested. Then they added, "Take two pictures of every good subject—and give us the better one."

Photographers responded generously. Dozens of striking color slides began to arrive at the Fenske house. "When a camera fan gives away his best pictures," Mrs. Fenske said gratefully, "that is really a deed far beyond the call of duty."

The volunteer committee members were themselves growing accustomed to performing beyond the call of duty. They worked long hours, some preparing mailings and stuffing envelopes, some in various town offices tracing owners of swamplands, checking land titles, and dickering for acreage whenever they had money on hand for a purchase. Other volunteers took on night assignments, seeing people in their homes to solicit their support, attending meetings and presenting their always popular slide talks. Mrs. Fenske recalls numerous occasions when, after serving dinner to her family, she had to rush out to present a slide talk before even removing the curlers in her hair.

"Mrs. Hand took them out for me while I drove us both to the meeting," she remembers.

In the meantime the well-financed Jersey Jet Site Association was waging its own aggressive battle on the political front. Its lobbyists approached state and local officials directly. Its lecturers, under the direction of its speakers' bureau, urged citizens to demand anti-jetport action of those same officials. And the Association was mounting a fund drive to raise $175,000 to further expand its work.

Compared to its highly publicized program, the efforts of the "bird watchers," as people often called the Great Swamp committee members, seemed gallant but ineffectual.

Nevertheless, in September of 1960, and with Dodge's generous help, the committee was able to offer the federal government some 1,000 acres of land on the condition that it be used for a natural wildlife refuge. The government reacted cautiously. The director of the Interior Department's Wildlife Bureau would not say if his bureau could accept the land in view of the Port Authority's announced plans for the swamp. Still the deeds to the land were left in the Bureau office, in a kind of escrow awaiting future developments, and the committee sent out a press release about its gift.

Suddenly many people who had scoffed good-naturedly at the "birdwatchers" began to think that the conservationists might after all actually achieve what the highly vocal anti-jetport organization was attempting. Though a thousand acres was apparently not enough to eliminate the jetport threat, it now occurred to the scoffers for the first time that the presentation of a larger area to the government might do the trick. Men and women who cared little about nature began to listen with some interest to appeals to help buy the Great Swamp. To them the volunteer conservationists began to look like the group that might beat the Port Authority.

The committee members themselves, however, still refused to characterize their campaign as an effort to thwart the Authority. To do so, they thought, would be dishonest, since their primary goal was saving the swamp—not defeating a government agency. They still believed in principle that they should stay out of the political controversy over the jetport. And, on a practical level, their tax-exempt status would be threatened if they became involved in politics. So in all their bulletins, news releases and speeches they continued to be careful, as they had been in the past, not even to mention the jetport. They talked about the importance of saving the swamp; and they talked about that alone.

But now, almost imperceptibly, their campaign took on a new aspect. It began to reach out to more segments of the population. It began to attract new volunteers who carried the campaign into new areas and provided it with new ammunition.

Slide lectures, originally presented by women speakers to women's groups, began to take place in men's organizations when influential men accepted some of the speaking assignments. The content of the talks changed too. Instead of concentrating on the swamp as a treasure trove for nature lovers, the speakers began to report on other qualities of the area they were trying to protect. Facts and figures and photographs presenting the role of the swamp as stabilizer of the local water resources found attentive listeners in men's clubs and service organizations. When a group of men heard a lecture on the importance of the swamp in reducing the danger of floods, none of them thought to label the speaker a bird watcher, even though he represented the Great Swamp Committee.

The committee also set out to arouse enthusiasm for its project among officials of the Fish and Wildlife Bureau. Letters and phone calls to John S. Gottschalk, the Bureau's regional director, produced an invitation to come to his Boston office for a half-hour meeting. Reluctant as they were to spend money on anything but land, and fearful that such a brief session could not justify any expenditure at all, the committee chairmen nevertheless had to authorize funds for an overnight stay in Boston, because Gottschalk had scheduled that meeting for eight-thirty in the morning.

On the day before their appointment the committee chairmen and Mrs. Fenske loaded a car with everything they thought might convince Gottschalk of their determination to save the swamp. There were brief-cases bulging with news releases and bulletins. There were containers of slide films. There were records of the near-200 slide talks committee members had already given. There were financial records, records of land bought and of purchases under negotiation. There were newspaper clippings to show the degree of local support the committee had received, and detailed maps of the swamp showing what had already been accomplished and what remained to be done.

Before the delegation had been in Gottschalk's office half its allotted time, Gottschalk was canceling other appointments for the rest of the morning so that he could go on listening to the story of the Great Swamp. Soon he was calling in his associates and introducing his visitors from Morris County as representatives of an outstandingly productive volunteer organization.

When the committee members left Boston they had no definite promise of active assistance, but they carried away the conviction that the regional director of the Wildlife Service believed the Great Swamp could—and would—be saved, and that he intended to give them every help in his power.

Some of that help was soon forthcoming. The manager of a nearby wildfowl refuge was given the part-time job of keeping an eye on the swamp and maintaining contact with the committee. Even more heartening was the announcement in May 1961 that the Department of the Interior would begin to survey the swamp as soon as 2,000 acres of it had been turned over to the government.

This announcement, of course, did not alter the necessity of acquiring at least 3,000 acres before the government could formally take over the land. It also did not alter the fact that by the summer of 1961 only 1,400 acres had been purchased—less than half of what would be needed to put the swamp beyond the reach of the Port Authority.

But if the committe had any doubts about being able to raise enough money to buy 1,600 more acres, it showed no signs of discouragement during the fall and winter of that year. It had grown in size as more and more volunteers offered their services. It had, in fact, outgrown its free headquarters in the Fenske kitchen, and rented modest quarters over the post office in the hamlet of New Vernon, on the edge of the swamp. Mrs. Fenske, however, continued to devote most of her time to committee work, although the work was no longer going on in her own home. She was able to do so because the salary of a baby-sitter for her young children had been judged a legitimate committee expense.

The Port of New York Authority sometimes, though involuntarily, aided the committee's efforts. Whenever an Authority spokesman issued a statement praising the swamp as a jetport site, the committee found its next morning's mail heavy with donations—evidence of the growing public belief that purchasing the swamp was the best way to block the jetport. During the summer of 1961, when the political pot was boiling in the state capital, and Governor Meyner was being picketed and booed for supporting the jetport scheme, the Great Swamp Committee enjoyed a small windfall.

Assistance of a different sort was coming at about the same time from a group of nearby colleges and universities. Members of the biology faculties of these schools, users of the swamp for many years, banded together to survey its natural assets. Much of the staggering array of material they collected, along with the results of James Hand's 10-year survey of the swamp's wildfowl, was sent to the Fish and Wildlife Bureau, both to inform the experts there and to impress them with the swamp's richness.

The teachers reported that there were 175 species of wildfowl in the swamp, and a remarkable animal population including white-tail deer, raccoon, muskrat, fox, mink and otter. Their list of swamp plants was long, and dramatically illustrated the swamp's uniqueness from an ecological point of view: investigators had proved it to be the farthest-south home of certain plants native to the northern United States, and the farthest-north home of other plants native to the South. Among the stands of ancient trees in the area were white oaks from 300 to 500 years old. One great beech tree's trunk measured 14 feet around.

Wildlife Bureau scientists thereafter sometimes called upon those college faculties for specific information. Once they asked for a survey of the acidity of brook water in various parts of the swamp. The assignment fell to the biology department of the College of St. Elizabeth. Two of the nuns on its teaching staff, in long habits which considerably complicated the task of collecting water samples, sent off the required information within a few days. The bureau scientists declared later that they had rarely if ever encountered such enthusiastic and satisfactory response to one of their requests.

As if to mark the committee's second anniversary, in the fall of 1961—at a time when 1,000 of the required 3,000 acres still remained unpurchased—two heartening events occurred. One was the arrival of federal surveyors to map the swamp, and to establish the boundaries of the areas already turned over to the Department of the Interior. The other was the arrival of a crew of men armed with shovels and posts, and with signs that read: THIS LAND IS BEING ACQUIRED BY THE CITIZENS OF NEW JERSEY AS A NATIONAL WILDLIFE REFUGE. Neatly lettered at the bottom of each sign were the words, U. S. DEPT. OF THE INTERIOR. The signs were a public signal that the Great Swamp Committee had the blessing of the government, and that the swamp would be a welcome addition to the nation's wildlife refuges.

Not long afterward, early in 1962, the biology faculties of four universities and five colleges, in a joint letter to Gottschalk, threw the full weight of their institutions' prestige into the fight to save the swamp. Their letter wholeheartedly endorsed the idea of creating a refuge in the swamp, and also pointed

106

out the area's specific value to the educational institutions of the region. The Great Swamp Committee, of course, made sure that the press reported the educators' letter, as it had already reported the survey the scientists had made, and Gottschalk's praise of the committee's efforts in an address to the National Audubon Society.

The Great Swamp Committee was discovering, however, that in some ways its recent successes added up to an obstacle. The new signs, and the presence of the surveying crews, led some people to believe that the committee had already attained its goal except, perhaps, for a few mopping-up operations; and those people regarded further contributions to the committee as unnecessary.

The committee was also losing support because feelings against the jetport had become so widespread that both major candidates for the governorship, and most members of the state legislature, were pledged to oppose it; and thus many people who had backed the committee's campaign purely as an anti-jetport measure, and who now believed the jetport would be blocked by political means, lost interest in the future of the swamp itself.

The Great Swamp Committee faced up to these new difficulties in the only way it knew. It worked harder than ever. It strove to win new converts to an appreciation of the swamp as a scientific classroom, as a shelter for plants and animals, as an aid to maintaining the balance of nature so easily disturbed by population and industrial growth, and as a haven of peace and quiet for millions of metropolitan residents.

Sometimes help came from unexpected sources. One day, for example, the committee heard of two high school seniors who had been making sound recordings and motion pictures of life in the swamp. Hoping to make use of their material, several committee members interviewed the boys—and realized almost instantly that these were no ordinary young men casually pursuing a hobby. Both boys were intent on careers in science. Both were seriously studying the swamp's flora and fauna. Both had amassed an amazing amount of knowledge of the swamp and what it contained. And both were eager to do all they could to preserve it.

Soon the boys were prime attractions of the committee's speaker service. Using their films and sound tapes, and describing in their own words the sensation of prowling deep inside the swamp's fastnesses, they appeared before service club luncheons, garden club meetings, and school assemblies. So infectious was their enthusiasm that businessmen who had never before given the swamp a serious thought found themselves working for its preservation. Schoolchildren took up collections to help the campaign. Garden club members, many of whom had given money for land purchases more than once, contributed still another time after hearing the boys speak.

In an effort to help the public develop a close relationship with the swamp, the committee devised a

"Buy an Acre of Swamp" campaign. Any person or group contributing $200 was considered to have bought an acre of swampland for the wildlife refuge. Large organizations bought several acres. Smaller groups purchased single acres. Boys and girls clubbed together to buy a fraction of an acre. Each purchaser, large buyer or small, individual or group, received a certificate from the North American Wildlife Foundation. Each could feel a personal stake in the future of the swamp. Visitors began to turn up at the committee's headquarters asking to look at the swamp of which they were now co-owners.

By the fall of 1962, when the committee was nearing the end of three years of work, 900 acres of land still had to be acquired. But the committee members were still hopeful. The government surveying teams had completed their job—a year of work in almost impassable morasses. Other government employees were already laboring in just-as-impassable legal morasses, trying to verify the often confusing land deeds and titles to the acreage already turned over to the government.

Hope was strong that by the following spring the goal might be won. And in that hope the committee had the open support not only of Gottschalk but of the Secretary of the Interior himself. Both men came to Morris County that fall to express their admiration of what the committee was doing.

In October Gottschalk addressed the Summit Nature Club, one of the committee's staunchest supporters. He talked about the plans for developing the swamp, about proposed easy-to-follow trails for the general public, sections to be set aside primarily for the use of college biology and botany departments, feeding and nesting areas for migratory wildfowl, and structures from which the public could observe the swamp's wildlife without frightening away its birds and animals.

About a month later Interior Secretary Stewart L. Udall addressed a dinner given by the Great Swamp Committee itself. He spoke glowingly of the committee's work and the value of the future refuge.

"You realized the federal government is not so endowed as to be able to buy all the desirable open space," he said, "so you went ahead on your own initiative.

"Such actions deserve to be trumpeted throughout the land as an abiding example of effective citizen action," he declared. "I dare say Henry Thoreau would applaud and I know you will be heroes of a sort to your grandchildren whether you realize it now or not."

Donations to the land-buying fund spurted after both those events, as had happened before when prominent men spoke out on behalf of the swamp. After the Udall dinner one philanthropic foundation presented the committee with a $10,000 check. Several times that amount arrived by mail in the next week or two. But even after this welcome flow of money was added to the committee's account, another quarter of a million dollars remained to be raised if the 3,000-

acre requirement was to be met. And the committee felt a new sense of urgency at this moment, because Gottschalk had announced that he would place the 2,000 acres already acquired under the management and administration of the U. S. Fish and Wildlife Service the following spring. He had thus proved his faith in the committee—at a time when it was still far from meeting its requirement; and by this act of faith he had also burdened its members with a heavier sense of responsibility than they had ever felt before.

The completion of a new Morris County shopping center, the Short Hills Mall, suggested a new way of appealing for help. Many Short Hills residents, owners of luxurious homes on large and small estates, had already made contributions to the committee. Some of their gifts had been sizable. But the committee members saw a chance of further assistance from the same people if the story of the swamp could somehow be brought more effectively to their attention. They thereore conceived the idea of borrowing the window of an empty store in the shopping center, and setting up in it a Great Swamp exhibit.

A little research resulted in the information that the Mall was owned by a large insurance company. Mrs. Fenske made an appointment with the company's agent, explained the committee's goal to him, and asked for the use of the store window for a short time. She was offered the window and the entire 90-foot-long store behind it.

Dazed by her success, she was on her way back to

the committee office before she began to wonder what
kind of an exhibit the committee could devise to fill
such an enormous display case.

"Fortunately we have a great deal of talent and
ability in this area," she said afterward. "We com-
mandeered most of it before that exhibit was ready."

Mrs. Robert MacPhail, an arts teacher turned
housewife, shaped and tied bundles of excelsior into
strikingly lifelike figures of swamp birds and animals.
Each was subtly colored with sprayed paint, and
mounted in a natural setting made of grass, leaves,
brush and other swamp materials.

Huge photographs, toned sepia and mounted on
cork backgrounds, illustrated the beauty and seren-
ity of the swamp, and the opportunities it offered for
study or quiet contemplation.

"The commercial price for those photographs would
have been prohibitive," Mrs. Fenske remembers. "But
we persuaded a friendly photographer to make them
for just the cost of the materials."

The committee persuaded more than 350 other
people to help, too. Some collected the material Mrs.
MacPhail needed from the swamp. Some built the
exhibit frames for the photographs and charts and
maps. Wives borrowed trucks from their husbands'
businesses to transport display materials to the workshop set up in the MacPhail cellar, and then to the
Short Hills Mall.

The display was a success, from the first moment
of the preview arranged for the press by the Summit

Garden Club. Many people who arrived in a mood of barely courteous attention stayed to marvel and exclaim over the figures, the photographs, and the informative captions and charts and maps that surrounded them.

Shoppers who glanced through the window in idle curiosity were almost invariably drawn inside. Many later returned with their husbands and children. Teachers came back for a second visit, bringing whole classrooms of children. Altogether some 30,000 viewers saw the exhibit before it was dismantled, and took away from it a better understanding of the swamp and the reasons for wanting to preserve it.

One visitor proved to be of special importance to the committee. He was a corporation lawyer, experienced in the ways of raising money for worthwhile causes. As the husband of a Summit Garden Club member, he had known a good deal about the Great Swamp Committee's efforts. But until he saw the exhibit, and talked with some of the committee members, he had not realized the scope of the group's activities. Now, impressed by its accomplishments, and by the dedication of the volunteer workers, he offered to help them raise the sum they still needed to buy the last 900 acres.

The chief targets of his efforts were the potentially big contributors, both private and corporate, and he persuaded a number of his influential friends to aid him. He was particularly careful when he chose an emissary to solicit a contribution from a corporation.

"When you're going to send someone to see a company president," he told Mrs. Fenske, "you'd better send a company president."

Large checks soon began to arrive at the committee office. Some of them were very large. Mrs. Fenske recalls opening the mail one morning and being jubilant at the sight of one contribution.

"Look at this!" she said. "A check for $5,000!" and passed the slip of paper across the table to the committee secretary.

The secretary's eyes opened wide. She handed the check back. "Look at it again, Helen," she said. "You didn't count all the zeros. That's $50,000!"

In two and one-half months the goal was reached. The last quarter of a million dollars the committee needed had arrived in its office.

Gottschalk was true to his word. In the spring of 1963 a manager was appointed and work crews began to lay out trails for students, bird watchers, wild flower enthusiasts, and people who simply like to walk through the world of nature. New signs were put up, each bearing the flying goose emblem of the Fish and Wildlife Service, each identifying the area as the Great Swamp National Wildlife Refuge.

In actuality the Refuge was still unborn. The committee, though proceeding as quickly as possible, was encountering a variety of obstacles in purchasing the land it could now afford to buy. Owners of certain parcels, who had perhaps inherited the property and never even seen it, were sometimes difficult to trace.

Deeds badly drawn were not easily transferred. Certain owners were reluctant to sell, for one reason or another, and others believed they could get a higher price if they hung on to their acres for another few months or years.

When 2,700 acres had been transferred to government ownership, the committee sent a delegation to Washington.

"We have the money for the remaining 300 acres," the delegates told Department of Interior officials, "but we haven't been able to complete their purchase. Will you accept the money instead and buy the land yourselves?"

They believed the government would have less difficulty than they were having in buying the land. But no one had ever made such a proposal to the Interior Department before. It had to be discussed at conferences and argued over at meetings. At last the Department's decision was reported to the committee: the government could not take the money, but it would proceed with the establishment of the Great Swamp Wildlife Refuge even though it had only 2,700 of the required 3,000 acres in hand. It trusted the committee to obtain the final 300 acres at its own best speed.

And so, on May 29, 1964, four and one-half years of work culminated in the formal dedication of the Great Swamp National Wildlife Refuge. The ceremony took place outside the swamp, at the estate of Marcellus Hartley Dodge, the man who had given so much toward preserving the swamp, but who had not lived to see its preservation assured by the government. The estate grounds were crowded. The speakers' stand was filled with dignitaries—Secretary Udall, Governor Richard Hughes, senators, congressmen, representatives of conservation organizations, officials of the Wildlife Service. There were so many dignitaries, in fact, that the members of the Great Swamp Committee were lost in the crush, unnoticed by most of the people who had gathered to celebrate a historic occasion.

But the day belonged to the committee members nevertheless. When Secretary Udall announced that over a million dollars had been contributed to the cause by 6,100 individuals and 462 organizations, foundations and industries, and that the money had come in from 289 towns in 29 states, he was reading cold figures. To the members of the Great Swamp Committee, each of those figures had a vivid reality. They had lived out the acquisition of every single one of those million dollars.

"It is the distinctive nature of this battle that makes the Great Swamp victory so important," the Secretary said, "for we applaud not action by the federal government or some public-spirited philanthropist or foundation, but disciplined, tough-minded action by voluntary citizen groups determined that the outdoors need not be sacrificed to demands of development."

The committee members smiled at each other over his use of the word disciplined, because they had always been self-conscious over what they considered the disorganization of their amateur efforts. But they accepted his reference to tough-minded action without question. They knew it had been precisely their tough-mindedness, their determination, which had served them as the best weapon in their long battle.

That day of dedication did not end their work. Eventually the committee purchased those last 300 acres. Then, re-formed into the North Jersey Conservation Foundation, it began to help the government increase its landholdings in the swamp to a total of some 6,000 acres, 3,750 of which were designated in 1968 as a National Wildlife Refuge Wilderness. It also began to publish a magazine, *Footprints,* designed to educate the public to the importance of conserving all the nation's natural resources. It set about buying, and stimulating other organizations to buy, additional land throughout northern New Jersey for parks and recreation areas. In cooperation with other organizations, such as service clubs, it set up a program of organized tours through the parks and conservation areas of the region. It offered ready assistance and advice, out of its own experience, to other groups of conservation-minded citizens fighting to protect natural resources from the bulldozer and the power shovel.

It continued, in short, to do what comes very naturally to dedicated citizens who believe that future generations have a right to inherit at least some of the open space that still remains in the once green and virgin land of America.

4

Campaigner for Economic Equality
LEON SULLIVAN

If Philadelphia's business executives had conducted an unpopularity contest in 1961 or 1962, the winner would almost certainly have been the Reverend Leon H. Sullivan, militant mainspring of a boycott movement to force open new job opportunities for Negroes. Yet only a few years later, in April, 1966, those same executives joined in applauding this Negro pastor of the Zion Baptist Church when he received the Philadelphia Award, highest honor the city can bestow.

What had happened in the intervening years was not that Sullivan had abandoned his fight for more and better jobs for Negroes; on the contrary, he had proved it could be won to the benefit of both the white business community and the underemployed blacks. The unique job-training program he had devised—

best known by the initials OIC, for Opportunities Industrialization Center—was already knocking sizable
holes in the educational and emotional walls that had
long kept American Negroes everywhere from a fair
share of America's affluence. That OIC program was
also breaching the equally formidable walls of misconceptions with which so much of the white business
community had surrounded itself—misconceptions
about the Negro's employment potential and his will
to work.

The Philadelphia *Bulletin* reported that the Reverend Sullivan wept as he accepted the Philadelphia
Award for outstanding public service. Perhaps the
sight surprised some of the many business executives
who had come up against Sullivan's rocklike determination during negotiating sessions. But by then most
Philadelphians, black and white, rich and poor, were
accustomed to being surprised by this six-foot five-
inch minister who had grown up on a dirt alley among
the back streets of Charleston, West Virginia.

Born in 1922, Leon Howard Sullivan was the only
child of parents who separated when he was three.
But so many aunts and uncles and young cousins
shared his mother's home that children sometimes
slept there three or four to a room. The house stood
close to the railroad tracks. Chairs and tables rattled
when the trains went by.

The boy's mother worked as an elevator operator
in an office building. Henry Parsons, who became his
stepfather, was a janitor in a small theater.

"My mother was a woman of very strong character who encouraged me to make the best of myself," Sullivan recalls today. "My stepfather was wonderful too. . . . He helped me all he could."

On holidays young Leon sometimes helped his stepfather at the theater, so that Henry Parsons could get off a little earlier than usual.

"We were poor, but we never went hungry," Sullivan says. "My people always worked. During the Depression we got mustard greens out of the yard and tomatoes from beside the railroad tracks—tomatoes that had fallen from boxcars."

He has vivid recollections of his teachers at the all-black schools he attended. "Those people were amazing," he says. "A great deal of the Negro's push for a better life came from the Southern teachers. They taught us to see goals beyond ourselves, beyond personal success. They taught Negro history and it became part of our thinking. . . . Looking back, I sometimes feel the kids in the North have missed something of the inspiration we had from our teachers. In the North, you don't always know what you are fighting because racial problems are veiled by hypocrisy. In the South, you always knew."

He knew clearly enough on such occasions as the day he walked into a drugstore to buy a Coke, and sat down on a counter stool.

"Get up from there, black boy, and stand on your feet," the proprietor ordered.

Sullivan, just thirteen years old at the time, translated the rough command into a piece of valuable advice. "I determined right there and then to stand on my own feet for the rest of my life," he says.

The militancy he was thus developing—which resulted, among other things, in his being the first Negro to use the Kanawha County Library—had deep roots in the religion he had learned at Sunday school and from his devoutly religious grandmother. He expressed it in the poetry he was beginning to write. He called one verse "The Lord's Answer."

> Oh, Lord, when You was making folks
> Why did I have to be?
> Of all the things to make for earth
> Why did You make a "me"?
> Then—coming through
> The blue of day
> A second voice
> Was heard to say:
> I know you're faring mighty hard,
> I know you're treated low.
> And, too, I know that better times
> Are coming mightly slow . . .
> But, son, they're coming.

His teachers liked his poetry and his eagerly questioning mind. "He didn't just swallow everything the teacher said, hook, bobber and sinker," one recalled of him years later. "He was always challenging in class. . . . He was the sort who makes good teachers because he kept them on their toes."

Talking once about his four years at Charleston's

Garnet High School, Sullivan said. "I ran for Boys' State in my senior year and was elected governor after I made some speeches, and read some of my poetry. The theme? Colored people getting up and getting free.

"That was, of course, the Negro Boys' State," he added. "The white boys elected their own governor. In those days the white boys would walk on the right side of the road and the Negroes on the left side and the only time we met was on Halloween night when we had a fight."

As a too-tall skinny young boy his long neck had earned him the nickname of Geese, which he hated. But by the time he was in high school his height helped make him the star center of the basketball team. He had filled out enough to play tackle on the football squad too. West Virginia State College offered him a full athletic scholarship. He arrived at the school with his total assets of $27.50 in his pocket.

He made the varsity football team in his freshman year. He became active on the student council, edited a journal of creative writing, and wrote more poetry as well as plays and short stories. His majors were psychology and sociology.

In his junior year he tore a leg ligament which still gives him trouble when he walks upstairs. He was forced to drop out of athletics. His scholarship was canceled.

He didn't even think of dropping out of school, however. Taking advantage of the wartime labor shortage, he found an eight-hour-a-day job in a steel mill 20 miles from college at a salary that would pay his expenses and tuition.

"It was a grind," he recalls now. "From nine A.M. to one P.M. I had classes. From four P.M. to midnight I worked at the plant. I'd get home at one thirty, study till three thirty, then sleep till eight."

The white workers at the steel plant soon began to worry about the big engaging youngster who put in a shift as long as their own, between a full morning of classes and hours of postmidnight study. Whenever possible they sent him off to a quiet corner to snatch a little extra sleep.

"I learned in those days that cooperation between whites and Negroes was possible, and I have never forgotten it," he says.

Aided by that cooperation, he somehow managed, during his senior year, to serve as president of his fraternity and of the student council, and to preach on Sundays at small Baptist churches in the nearby towns of Vandalia and Montgomery.

By then he was already firmly committed to the ministry, though today he can no longer remember when he first felt, as he puts it, that "I could help my people best by being a pastor." He does clearly recall the important role played in his life by the Reverend Moses Newsome of Charleston.

"He schooled me, licensed me and gave me my real chance," Sullivan says of the man who helped him become a minister before he was eighteen years old.

Who Says You Can't?

One day Sullivan read that the Reverend Adam Clayton Powell was coming to Charleston to speak. Powell was not yet active in politics, but he was already widely known as pastor of the large Abyssinian Baptist Church in New York's Harlem. Sullivan, who knew that Powell's parents had once lived in Montgomery, wrote asking the prominent Negro church leader to visit that little West Virginia town before returning North, and to address the congregation Sullivan served there. Powell came, and was so impressed with his young host that he offered Sullivan his help if he ever came to New York.

Sullivan landed in New York not long afterward. A scholarship sponsored jointly by Columbia University and Union Theological Seminary permitted him to work toward a master's degree in religious education. He was able to support himself while he studied because Powell kept his word. Through his influence Sullivan became the first Negro ever hired by the Bell Telephone Company to collect coins from pay telephones.

"He was a real West Virginia mountaineer—tall and gangly and scared to death because he'd never been in the big city before," Powell said of him afterward. "I told him, 'You look like you never put on shoes before,' but I had faith in him . . . and the number one thing you felt about him was his integrity."

As a theological student Sullivan served as pastor of a small Presbyterian church in Harlem, and shared in the ferment of the burgeoning civil rights movement. When Powell was about to run for the first of his many terms as a New York Democratic Congressman, on a platform demanding more rights for Negroes, he asked Sullivan to become his assistant at the Abyssinian Baptist Church. Sullivan kept that post until he took his degree and was invited to minister to the First Baptist Church of East Orange, New Jersey. He went there with his Baltimore-born bride, and was soon elected to the Council of Churches. Again he was breaking new ground. There had never been a Negro on the East Orange Council before.

In 1950 Sullivan received the call that took him to Philadelphia, to the Zion Baptist Church. Its 600 members—who would soon increase to 5,000 under his leadership—lived in a low- to moderate-income neighborhood notable for its high crime rate. They were scarcely accustomed to being a focus of admiring national attention. But their church was about to become known throughout the country as the foundation stone of the revolutionary community projects inaugurated by their towering young pastor.

The first of those projects grew out of Sullivan's deep concern over the problem of juvenile delinquency. Soon after his arrival he began spending a lot of time on street corners. ("That's where he found me," one OIC project director says. "He picked me up off the street. I'd probably still be there today if it weren't form him.") Somehow Sullivan was able to get through to troubled young people, to drug addicts, to alcoholics. No effort ever seemed too great for him if it opened up communication with someone he thought needed help: He once learned sign language so that he could communicate with the deaf.

Before long he was heading a citywide committee set up with the specific purpose of combating delinquency among Philadelphia youth. His effectiveness was so widely recognized that in 1955 he was named by the Junior Chamber of Commerce as one of the ten most outstanding young men in the United States.

But Sullivan himself was by no means satisfied with what had been accomplished, especially on the level of finding jobs for the city's idle youth, among whom Negroes far outnumbered whites.

"Thousands of Negro boys and girls were walking the streets of Philadelphia unable to obtain jobs," he once told an interviewer, "while white boys and girls who had graduated from the same high schools were working."

Determined to tackle head on this root cause of delinquency and despair, he set up a Youth Employment Service in the basement of the Zion Baptist Church. The young man he asked to direct it was the Reverend Thomas J. Ritter, pastor of another Philadelphia Baptist church since his graduation from theological school only two years earlier.

The two men, one so strikingly big, the other slight and quick, understood each other and understood the need they were trying to meet. "We were both brought up poor," Ritter says.

Born in South Carolina, the fourth of seven children, Ritter had been moved North soon afterward, when his father went to Pennsylvania to seek work. After finishing high school, and taking some extension courses at the state university, he spent two years during World War II in the Army, studied pharmacy for a time, and then worked as partner with the Ritter Brothers' Medical Equipment Sales Company before deciding to go into the ministry. He was already deeply concerned with community problems when Sullivan enlisted his help.

The new employment center found jobs for about 1,000 young Negroes a year. Sullivan remained dissatisfied. More thousands of young people in Philadelphia's Negro slums were still unemployed. Furthermore many of those who had been placed were working only part time, and almost all of them at the kinds of menial job then commonly reserved for Negroes—jobs as janitors, sweepers, handymen, dishwashers, laundresses and domestic servants. Sullivan wanted more jobs for his young people, and better jobs. He particularly wanted what he called "sensitive" jobs as clerks, typists, salesmen, receptionists and telephone operators. Because the holders of such jobs dealt directly with the white public, and shared rest rooms and lunchrooms with white co-workers, those jobs were invariably given only to whites.

The time had come, Sullivan believed, to battle the discrimination which locked Negroes out of so large an area of employment. And it seemed to him that a powerfully effective weapon for the battle lay ready to hand: the buying power of the 27 percent of Philadelphia's population that was black.

In March, 1960, he met with some 15 other Negro ministers of the city. No executive committee or board of directors was chosen, either then or at any later time. Those present simply discussed what came to be called a Selective Patronage campaign. It purpose was to withhold Negro patronage first from one company and then from another, until each company in its turn met certain specific demands on Negro employment.

That small meeting was the beginning of what Sullivan has described as "the best organized unorganized venture in the country." He was recognized as its architect; both the policy of concentrating on a single company at a time and the lack of formal organization represented his thinking. But neither he nor any of the 400 ministers eventually involved in the campaign ever claimed its leadership. Each one led only his own congregation in what was essentially a boycott movement, though the word "boycott" was never used by its participants.

Sullivan had elected to work with and through the men of his own profession because they made up, in his words, "the only morally organized network of communication in the Negro community." He was convinced that the Selective Patronage drive, to be effective, "would have to have a moral as well as a mass base." And he believed that ministers were the ones who could most authoritatively ask people to stop—or start—buying the products of a specific company.

Of course plans had to be made, and so a sort of shadowy steering committee evolved, without a chairman or a regular schedule of meetings, and with a membership that changed frequently. Nevertheless its plans were definite. It decided that the baking industry would be the campaign's first target, and that the company within that industry to be tackled first was one specializing in moderate-priced packaged goods.

The first step in the campaign was taken without fanfare. A small delegation of ministers—four or five men—called on the company's executives. Courteously they asked questions about the company's operations and its employment policies; they asked particularly about the number of Negroes it employed, and in what capacities. They were answered with equal courtesy. The meeting was amicable.

"We always laughed and joked with the industry leaders we visited," Ritter recalled later. "And when we left, we said we'd be back the next week."

They did return the following week, armed this time with a list. "We would like to see Negroes in all these jobs," they said. The list ranged over a wide field of skilled and semiskilled occupations, including clerical, selling, machine operation and maintenance jobs.

The ministers stated clearly that what they were making at that moment was merely a token request to give the company an opportunity to demonstrate its goodwill. They also said that the Negro community would not be fully satisfied with a token response, but would expect the hiring of Negroes to continue until Negroes held a fair share of the better jobs available in the company.

The executives responded—at that and at subsequent meetings in other company offices—in ways that could have been predicted.

They said they already employed many Negroes. To that the ministers replied that they were not concerned solely with quantity, but also with quality; that the mass employment of Negroes in menial jobs was not enough; that Negroes must be hired to fill specific "sensitive" positions.

An executive who claimed that a union contract mandated the rehiring of recently laid-off workers, before any new employees could be hired, was told that this was an obstacle to be surmounted by the company itself, not by the Negro community.

A sales director who stated that Negroes in selling positions would offend white customers was politely reminded that the company was already offending more than one-quarter of the residents of Philadelphia by failing to hire Negroes for such jobs.

The clergymen then named the specific period of time within which they expected their list of jobs to be filled, and the second meeting ended.

Up to that point there had been no publicity. Nor was any announcement made to the press when the time period ended and the company had failed to fulfill the ministers' requirements. But on the following Sunday every minister in Sullivan's group had a special message for his congregation.

"After we talked about God, we talked about the company," Sullivan once put it.

Each of them prefaced his message with his own version of Sullivan's statement: "We cannot, in good moral conscience, remain quiet while our people patronize companies that discriminate against our people."

Then each minister asked his congregation to cease buying the products of the baking company until its discriminatory policies were abandoned.

The response was immediate. Women, normally the most regular churchgoers, as well as the usual purchasers of baked goods, listened to their pastors' words and realized they were not being asked to do anything which they could not easily do. They were not, after all, being urged to stop buying all baked goods, but merely the products of a single company. With the enthusiasm of people playing a new game, and one that gave them a sense of cooperating for the benefit of their own people, they let the products of that company go stale on the shelves of every small grocery and huge supermarket in their various neighborhoods.

For a time the company made no move. Perhaps its executives believed the campaign would soon wear itself out, that people would grow tired of it or forget it. But that didn't happen. The women might have forgotten, or wearied of checking the maker's name on every package of baked goods they picked up, but each Sunday they were reminded again of the campaign's importance and the potential good it could accomplish.

At the end of eight weeks the company capitulated, no longer able to bear the loss of its Negro customers. And the other baking companies in the area hastily complied with the job requests then made to them. Each had seen the effects of the first Selective Patronage campaign, and was eager to avoid becoming the next victim.

The ministers then moved on to a second industry, and a third. Their unorganized group held together largely because of its success, but partly for the very reason that it was unorganized. No man, not even the minister of the city's smallest storefront church, felt that he was taking orders from another. And as the leaders of large wealthy congregations worked month after month with the storefront ministers they had tended to look down on, they all felt a new solidarity in their common effectiveness and in the new role they had assumed in the lives of their parishioners.

"For the first time," Ritter explains, "the ministers had come to mean more to the Negro community than its successful lawyers, doctors, and businessmen. And under the leadership of the united clergy something happened that had not happened before. The entire black community solidified—the wealthiest professionals, the middle class, and the poorest workers all came to understand a common purpose."

Something else happened as a result of the meetings between ministers and industrial leaders. "We established a new bridge with industry," Ritter says. "We started a dialogue that had never existed before. We all found we had things to say that were worth listening to."

Some Selective Patronage campaigns took longer than others. One against an ice-cream manufacturer seemed permanently stalled, in spite of the fact that Negro parishioners assured their pastors they were not buying the company's products. Then a survey pinpointed the trouble: Children were buying the ice cream at school. Word went out to the Negro schoolchildren and sales then dropped off so abruptly that victory was assured.

Another campaign, against the manufacturer of a famous soft drink, ended in a swift two weeks, to no one's surprise. "After all," Ritter points out, "almost half of that company's total Philadelphia sales came from the Negro neighborhoods."

Negro sales represented a far smaller part of most companies' incomes, but in every case they proved numerous enough to make the difference between profit and loss. Thus one company after another gave in to the Negro ministers' demands. And usually a campaign against one company in an industry was enough; the rest fell eagerly and quickly into line.

The animosity directed toward the ministers by white industrialists, during the early days of the boycotts, was aimed chiefly at Sullivan. He paid little attension to the warning or threatening phone calls he received, but he could not be unaware of the strong feeling against him. "They hated my guts," he recalled later.

But gradually the attitude of the businessmen changed. They were discovering that none of the evils they had anticipated, as a result of their enforced new employment practices, actually came to pass. Their white workers did not suffer any loss of morale when skilled Negroes went to work alongside them. They did not stage mass walkouts when Negroes shared their washrooms and lunchrooms. White clients seemed equally undisturbed. A white housewife apparently demanded nothing but efficient, courteous and friendly service from a department store clerk; she was not in the least concerned about the color of the clerk's skin.

Once they became aware of this, the businessmen's alarm gave way to a kind of pride in the new policy they had adopted with such reluctance but which was now winning them praise from various quarters. Their attitude toward the Reverend Sullivan reflected the change.

"They all began to love me," Sullivan recalls, "because suddenly they were big liberals. Nothing bad had happened, and we'd helped their public image."

By the end of 1962 twenty-nine Selective Patronage campaigns had won almost 4,000 skilled jobs for Philadelphia Negroes—and without, as Sullivan has pointed out, "a single picket line or sit-in or a penny spent on litigation." Those new jobs were few compared to the

70,000 unemployed Negroes in Philadelphia at the time. But the real significance of those twenty-nine campaigns was nevertheless important: They had proved that Negroes could do skilled work, and that the heavens did not fall when Negroes performed their jobs alongside white workers. The value of hiring Negroes for skilled work had in fact been so widely accepted that business and industry suddenly sought still more skilled black workers.

Sullivan realized that the new demand outstripped the supply.

"We had known long before we even started the Youth Employment Service that there was a desperate need to train Negroes for better jobs," Ritter says, recalling their reaction to the situation. "The need had been obvious then. We didn't need this new development to point it out to us. What did surprise us, though, was the speed with which the demand for trained Negroes was growing, as Philadelphia employers learned that it was good business to hire Negroes for skilled jobs."

In an effort to meet that demand, Sullivan immediately formed a research council, in the winter of 1962-63, to study the training and retraining programs then being conducted under government auspices throughout the country. By the following July he was ready to announce plans for what he called the OIC, the Opportunities Industrialization Center. He had no tangible assets at all—no money, no building, no teachers, no equipment. What he did have was ideas.

One of Sullivan's ideas was that if a training program were to succeed, it should be tied so closely to the people it served that those people would consider it their own. Therefore, while other job-training programs sought vast grants from various federal agencies, he sought his support from the Negro community of Philadelphia. Ministers who had once preached the doctrine of Selective Patronage now urged their parishioners to get behind the OIC.

Soon a small army of women was marching through Negro neighborhoods, soliciting funds from door to door. The women raised $50,000. Small businessmen in the Negro community raised an equal sum.

Calls for volunteer teachers brought 150 Negro technicians, engineers, scientists and craftsmen to an initial meeting, all of them willing to work in their spare time to staff the still-in-the-future OIC. By the fall of 1963 the number of volunteers had doubled, and included whites as well as Negroes.

Another of Sullivan's ideas was that industry too must become a partner in the OIC—not a silent partner giving merely its blessing and perhaps token financial aid, but an active partner actively engaged in the job-training program. Sullivan wanted industry to help him plan courses of instruction that would fit trainees for specific jobs that actually existed. He wanted industry to supply modern, currently in use production machinery and equipment on which trainees could learn the tasks they would be expected to perform on those jobs. He wanted industry to train his volunteer OIC teachers to instruct trainees in the use of that machinery and equipment.

In search of that kind of partnership Sullivan called on some of the city's most important industrialists and businessmen. His reputation for integrity and performance had preceded him, especially with those executives whose companies had been targets of the Selective Patronage campaigns. His report of the support the Negro community was already giving to the new project called forth their admiration. As practical men, aware of their need for skilled workers, the executives listened to Sullivan's plans for the OIC and decided it might produce those workers. One by one they pledged to him not only funds but machinery and equipment, textbooks and training manuals, and technical assistance.

In October the last big obstacle appeared to be overcome when the city agreed—at the urging of a Negro councilman—to lease the OIC a four-story building for $1 a year.

The building proved to be an old and derelict police station, however. Its basement was flooded ankle-deep. Its windows were shattered. Huge holes gaped in its floors. The plumbing, heating and electrical wiring systems were all beyond repair. Cost of rehabilitating the structure seemed prohibitive.

Then, as if to justify Sullivan's unshakable faith, an anonymous benefactor sent him a $50,000 donation. Work on the old building began immediately, carried out almost entirely by Negro plumbers, electricians, carpenters, masons and painters. The flooded basement was drained, waterproofed and readied to receive heavy factory machinery. Walls and iron bars were ripped out, and cells were converted into classrooms, offices and a kitchen equipped for the training of cooks and cooks' assistants. The roll room, where patrolmen had once stood inspection before going out on their rounds, became a restaurant bright with yellow paint. Other rooms were wired for electronic communication equipment, or fitted up as chemical laboratories and drafting rooms. Everything was done at top speed, with the fervor and enthusiasm of an old-fashioned barn raising. In January, 1964, a scant half year after Sullivan had announced the plans for the OIC, the center was dedicated before an enthusiastic crowd of 8,000. There were speeches and music and—because it was a cold day—hot coffee and doughnuts for everyone.

Some 4,500 persons immediately applied for instruction in the OIC's day and evening classes, scheduled to begin in March. Only 300 could be accommodated. Volunteer counselors selected that number by means of tests and interviews. There could be no doubt of the applicants' sincerity; unlike trainees in most government-sponsored programs, they knew they were expected to pay a fee of $25 for each course. (This fee, later abandoned and never required of anyone really unable to pay, was intended to bolster the trainee's self-respect, as well as to weed out those seeking pay for training rather than the training itself.)

As soon as classes began, the old building hummed with new activity. Students bent over power sewing machines, laboratory test tubes and electronic equipment. They worked among the cooking odors of the kitchen-practices section, and among the rattle of silverware and dishes in the restaurant-classroom. They stood beside heavy machines installed in the basement of the onetime police station.

"I'm a militant," Sullivan told a reporter who interviewed him later that year. "I've run demonstrations, and I may run them again. But right now I'm in the education business."

From some points of view the "business" seemed to be flourishing, owing to a $200,000 Ford Foundation grant. In other respects it was failing in the same way so many other job-training projects were failing at the same time: it had a high rate of dropouts. Students were leaving before they finished their courses, usually to return to the aimless and idle lives from which Sullivan and his staff had hoped to rescue them.

Sullivan had known from the start that the majority of the students enrolled in the program would be what he called "brainwashed"—conditioned to the belief that they were fit only for menial labor. He had hoped that plunging them into a training course designed to fit them for better jobs would overcome their sense of inferiority and give them confidence that they could improve their lives. Now he had come to realize that the will to succeed could not be so readily implanted.

He had also discovered the grim fact that many OIC

students totally lacked the basic skills essential for utilizing new training. Their median educational level was the eighth grade, but in actual fact many were barely literate and could not deal with figures at all. This meant not only that they could not absorb much of the information their teachers were trying to give them, but also that they would be unable to make good use of what they could learn. No man could become a restaurant cook, no matter how deft he showed himself in a kitchen, if he could not read and follow a recipe and figure his food costs. No girl could become a waitress who could not write out a customer's check.

To many people the number of dropouts from the OIC seemed proof that Sullivan had attempted the impossible when he set out to train even hard-core unemployed or underemployed to the point where they could handle skilled jobs. They told him, in effect, that he should have known he could not make silk purses out of sows' ears.

Sullivan wasn't listening. He and Ritter and their staff were too busy developing what would come to be recognized as the OIC's unique feature, and the one which has made it a model or dozens of other training programs. Its name, Feeder Program, describes its function. It is designed to feed into the OIC men and women already prepared, educationally and psychologically, to derive benefit from its training.

"Neither of us was a real educator," Ritter says, recalling the days when the Feeder Program was in its planning stage. "But I guess it was one of those times when ignorance was bliss. An expert might have said the approaches and techniques we planned to use wouldn't work. Not being experts, we just went ahead and made them work."

With additional funds from industry they opened in September, 1964, the new "school," which every trainee now attends before being admitted to actual OIC job training. Its function can probably best be understood by following an OIC applicant from the moment he first walks into the Feeder Program's North Philadelphia quarters. Perhaps he has been coaxed into it from a pool hall, by one of the OIC's recruiters. Perhaps he has wandered in on his own because he has met a former OIC trainee who now works happily at a well-paying skilled job.

The applicant—let's say his name is John Smith—is registered and assigned to a professional counselor, who will follow his progress from now on. His initial interview with the counselor is lengthy. It may require several sessions. During it the counselor learns a great deal about John's background, personality and capacities, and his hopes for the future. If he has any physical disability—poor eyesight, for example—he is sent to a clinic for treatment or correction. Finally John and the counselor agree on the particular job training John will undertake when he has completed the Feeder Program he is now about to enter.

If he already has a job, and wishes only to improve his work status and earning ability, he will probably attend classes in the evening. If he needs a temporary job for support during his training, he applies for it through the program's employment office. If he can devote his full time to training, he begins to attend daytime classes as soon as an opening is available. Since classes are kept small, and there is always a waiting list of students hoping to enter, he may have to wait some time for his chance.

One of the classes John takes, when he joins the program, is in communication skills. This term, which saves face for an adult student who may not want to admit his lack of literacy, is a euphemism—though an accurate one—for elementary reading and writing. If John is already adept at these skills, he will remain in this class only long enough to prove his ability to his teacher. If not, he will stay until he can read and write on at least a third-grade level. He also takes a course in computational skills—simple arithmetic. More advanced communications skills and computational skills will be a part of his actual job training.

In another class he learns something about his role as a consumer. He is urged to think realistically about the salary he expects to receive when his job training is completed, and how to budget that salary. In this class, as in all his others, he acquires experience in marshaling and articulating his thoughts.

If necessary, John attends a class in which English is taught as if it were a foreign language, as indeed it is for many of the Spanish-speaking Puerto Rican immigrants now enrolled in the OIC. Other special courses he may choose will prepare him to take civil service examinations, or to train for typing or laboratory work.

Among the courses that all students take is one in minority history which teaches them, as Sullivan explains it, about "their own roots that go deep down into history" and "to appreciate their contribution to American life."

There is, finally, a personal finishing class conducted in a mirror-walled room. There John's clothes, his posture and his mannerisms are as visible to him as to the other students, all of whom are expected to appear as neatly dressed as if they were daily facing a critical employer. Under the teacher's guidance they discuss the techniques of good grooming, of applying for a job, of generally getting along well with others and of creating a best-foot-forward impression in new situations. Like the entire program, this course is designed to give John not only practical information and skills, but also self-confidence and pride.

"We taught our girls," Sullivan said once in a speech "that they didn't have to be blond to be beautiful, and we taught our colored men that they did not have to be white to be smart. We taught our people to have respect for what they are, for we know that if a man gains respect for what he is, then there is no need for him to hate any more! We taught that genius is color blind. . . . We taught our people how to walk, how to sit, how to talk—but most of all in the Feeder Program we taught our people to put their heads up and their shoulders back. For we found that the greatest key to motivation is self-respect."

He visits the school often himself, and his presence as much as his words urge the students on to do their best. They know his story; they recognize it as a lesson in what determination and perseverance can accomplish. They know he means it when he says he is proud of them; it makes them proud of themselves.

A trainee with a good educational background and a strong sense of motivation may move out of the Feeder Program into a job-training program very quickly. A trainee poorly equipped for actual job training may remain in the program for six or eight months or even longer. Special care is taken that his classes are not permitted to become too academic, too formidable for someone struggling for literacy and fighting for self-respect. Ritter, the Feeder Program's executive director, says, "We want to give the students enough to let them function in the job they're after, but not enough to panic them."

Just how much that is each teacher must decide for every student—a decision complicated by the fact that a teacher is always dealing with a mixed group of students, some newly arrived in the class, others long-term enrollees. The choice demands great flexibility on the teacher's part, and the ability to relate directly and separately to each individual. Staffing the school is thus a matter of great concern to both Ritter and Sullivan. They must choose teachers and administrators who are capable of handling a constantly shifting student population. They must select counselors as warmly sympathetic as they are competent. All teachers, administrators and counselors must be able to coordinate their efforts when, for example, a student stops attending class; then that student must be sought out and helped, if possible, to overcome whatever emotional, financial or educational difficulty has turned him away from the opportunity the school offers him.

Every member of the staff, in other words, must share Sullivan's own devotion to the program's purpose, symbolized by the golden key he chose as its emblem. It is a skeleton key because, Sullivan explains, "A skeleton key opens all doors."

A student "graduated" from the Feeder Program goes on to specific job training as soon as a vacancy opens up in the course he has selected. He may learn any one of some thirty skills at one of the four OIC branches now functioning in various parts of the city. Each branch specializes in certain fields. At the North Branch, for example, he might learn machine tooling, welding, sheet metal work, drafting or restaurant practices; at the West Branch, electronics or secretarial skills; at the South Branch, clerical skills, printing, or graphic arts; at the Germantown Branch, laundry and dry cleaning, air-conditioning and refrigeration repair, power sewing, plumbing or brick masonry.

"Our people used to sweep the floors around the machines," Sullivan says. "Now they operate the machines."

And Ritter says, "I carried a hod for bricklayers when I was young—white bricklayers. Now black men are laying bricks too."

By 1968, as the OIC neared its fourth birthday, it employed more than 300 teachers and counselors, all well paid—the OIC no longer depends on volunteers— and was training 1,500 students at a time. Between 5,000 and 6,000 applicants normally awaited admission to the Feeder Program.

The Feeder Program was by then largely financed by the U.S. Department of Labor, and the OIC received other federal funds through the Office of Economic Opportunity. Business, industry and interested individuals also continued their aid to the program. (The OIC's West Philadelphia Branch is rented to the organization by a philanthropist who asks in return only an annual "fee" of one cup of black coffee and one slice of black bread—a fee that is ceremoniously paid to him each year.)

By 1968 the OIC graduates numbered about 5,000, most of them Negroes. Eighty percent of that number were already at work on jobs that utilized their new skills. Almost all had come originally from poverty-stricken homes; about one-third had been on relief rolls. Among the graduates, Sullivan points out, were some who had taken part four years earlier in destructive riots. The program which had grown out of his interest in the city's juvenile delinquents was regularly producing job-holding, tax-paying citizens.

"Of course we haven't done enough," Ritter says. "Everything we've accomplished is just a drop in the bucket compared to what still needs to be done."

"This is just a beginning," Sullivan says.

There were other beginnings by 1968 too, specifically in the OIC programs known as RISE and AAE.

RISE—the name is an acronym for Retraining for Industrial Social Service and Employment—had been undertaken at the request of the U.S. Department of Labor, which provided it with funds. Its purpose is to reach people who have been out of work so long that they have lost the will to seek a job, and people recently arrived in the city from rural areas, totally untrained and resigned to living indefinitely on welfare checks. RISE recruits them, puts them through a concentrated Little Feeder Program, and helps place them in factories where they receive on-the-job training. Graduates of the experimental RISE crash program must usually take unskilled jobs initially, but the increased self-respect that comes with their first paychecks often prompts them to seek further training through the OIC or some other advanced training program.

The AAE, or Adult Armchair Education program, reaches out into neighborhoods, where it conducts classes in the living rooms of people offering their homes for the purpose. Ten men and women, often unemployed or underemployed, are recruited for each class. Each class meets for ten weekly sessions, to discuss or study a subject of the members' own choosing. A teacher provides informal guidance. Some groups concentrate on reading and writing; others want to learn how to get better value for their consumer dollars, or how to solve a particular community problem.

Three thousand people attended classes in more than 300 homes in AAE's first year of operation. Some of those people, earlier fearful of any formal education, lost their timidity during the class sessions and went on to enroll in conventional adult-education or job-training programs. Others, stirred to new interest and a new sense of responsibility, moved toward roles of community leadership.

One more OIC project, the OIC Institute, was created when Sullivan and Ritter and their associates could no longer keep up with requests for information about their unusual—and unusually successful—program. Almost from the beginning they had been besieged by visitors eager to learn how the OIC program was set up. Some of the visitors were other ministers. Some were municipal, state and federal officials, and representatives of foreign lands. All were concerned with problems of unemployment and job training in their own areas. All hoped to find in the OIC a solution to some of those problems.

Sullivan had welcomed the guests and their queries and supplied them with all the information they sought. He had responded to correspondents seeking the same information. He and Ritter had also traveled widely at the invitation of business, industrial and governmental groups in various parts of the country, to speak about the OIC and its functions. But when federal funds were offered to establish an OIC information center, they turned over to it the major responsibility of expounding the OIC philosophy and demonstrating the techniques of establishing and operating the OIC prototypes. By 1968, with the institute's help, OIC programs were either fully developed or under development in sixty-five other cities.

The OIC had won recognition as one of the most hopeful methods ever devised for fighting poverty and despair, and for shattering the patterns of discrimination that help perpetuate those ills.

Sullivan has never considered his efforts to improve the Negro's economic lot as an extracurricular activity. To him it has always been an integral part of his work as pastor of the Zion Baptist Church.

"It's an outgrowth of my ministry," he has said, "of my efforts to make religion functional. I don't want to be the sort of minister who promises his people milk and honey in heaven. I want to offer them some ham and eggs here on earth."

Offering them ham and eggs, he believes, involves a good deal more than training people for better jobs and making such jobs available to them. It also involves seeing to it that Negroes share in the ownership and management of business and industrial enterprises, and thus acquire control of their own economic destiny.

His first move along those lines was made back in 1962, when the Selective Patronage campaign was still under way. It was then he invited his parishioners to join what he called the 10–36–50 club. It was to consist of 50 people—if he could convince that many to take part in it—who would each put $10 in an investment fund every month for 36 months. At the end of that time a decision would be made on what to do with the accumulated money.

Most people believed he would fail. They doubted that there was that much idle money among his parishioners, and that anyone would put money into a fund whose eventual use was unknown. Even Sullivan was surprised when he found himself almost at once with more than 200 investors and more signing up every day. The name of the organization had to be changed immediately to 10–36. By the end of one year there was enough money in the fund to start putting it to work.

Sullivan had always known in a general way what he wanted the money to accomplish. He wanted part of it to finance better housing for Negroes, and the rest to be invested in business and industrial enterprises managed and staffed by Negroes. And during that year he had met frequently with a small group of young men to work out the details of a program.

Three of those young men became executives in the enterprises that grew out of their meetings and the Zion Church funds. One of them, Elmer H. Young, Jr., now Sullivan's administrative assistant for Zion investments, recalls the problem he faced when Sullivan offered him a job.

"I'd gone from Temple University School of Business Administration to a position with IBM," he says. "And I'd been with IBM for ten years when the Reverend Sullivan asked me to join him. It took some thinking about, and a lot of talking with my wife. My job at IBM paid well, and gave me the fringe benefits of a good insurance and pension plan and stock-buying privileges. And here I was being asked to give that all up for a job that paid less and had a future that depended completely on faith.

"But we didn't have much choice, really," he concludes, "when we were faced with the Reverend Sullivan's determination and *his* faith, and his selfless dedication. He doesn't accept any salary from any of the organizations he has created and watches over, you know. The only salary he takes is the one from the church. And since we felt he was right in what he was trying to do—well, there wasn't anything else for me to do but join up."

The plans, when finally crystallized, called for the formation of two investment corporations. One, the Zion Non-Profit Corporation, was dedicated to building new housing in Negro communities. The other, the Zion Investment Associates, Inc., was to be a profit-making investment firm whose profits were to be distributed as follows: 40 percent to the investors, 40 percent to community development, and 20 percent to its employees in the form of bonuses.

The Zion Non-Profit Corporation was in business first. It spent $21,000 on feasibility studies and plans for a ninety-six-unit low- and middle-income garden apartment complex. "We wanted to give the future tenants the kinds of luxuries and attractive surroundings they had never had before," Young recalls. "So

151

we included air conditioning and garbage disposal units and we planned on bright colors—yellow for kitchen walls and appliances, for example."

When the plans were complete, the corporation applied for a government-guaranteed mortgage, and was lent $1,000,000—the total cost of the project. Workmen, many of them recent OIC building trades graduates, were soon swarming over the site. And long before the first of the two planned buildings was completed, late in 1966, more than 500 families had applied for its forty-eight apartments.

Among the projects undertaken by the Zion Investment Associates was the construction of a $1,700,000 shopping center in the heart of North Philadelphia's Negro ghetto. Its success was assured before it was built. Four or five prospective tenants had applied for each available shop.

Another profit-making venture of the associates is the Progress Garment Manufacturing Company, established with the active support and cooperation of both the International Ladies Garment Workers Union and the Villager Corporation, producer of women's clothes. The latter provided a four-month course to teach OIC-trained power-sewing graduates the specific techniques of turning out Villager skirts, and a one-month course to train the new factory's supervisory personnel.

Still another associates project is the Progress Aero-Space Enterprises, producer of components for space vehicles. The General Electric Corporation supplied the manufacturing unit with machinery, technical advice and worker training, and then demonstrated its full confidence in the new venture by giving it a $2,500,000 contract for electronic parts.

"Black talent manages this plant," Young says, "but we have an integrated production staff. After all, we don't think America should have a black road and a white road. And we don't intend to do to the white man what he has done to us."

The Reverend Sullivan had a special reason for wanting to see Progress Aero-Space come into being, a reason born out of the realism and idealism that coexist in his heart and mind.

"When the first spaceship lands on the moon," he said when the company was being established, "we want it to have something in it that *we* made. We want to prove we can do difficult things."

Thousands of people who have benefited directly from his help and his work, and many thousands more who have only heard of him, agree that the "difficult things" the Reverend Sullivan has accomplished provide dramatic proof that he himself has succeeded in reaching that goal.

5

Crusader for Literacy

DANIEL FADER

Daniel Fader, Renaissance scholar and professor of English language and literature at the University of Michigan, is an educator who thinks most English teachers don't teach English. He says so loudly and often.

Just as audibly he regrets the public's inability to hold those teachers accountable for their failure. "A doctor or a lawyer who makes an error can be sued for malpractice," he has said. "There is no such thing as a malpractice suit against a teacher who teaches badly. All a teacher gets for bad teaching, year after year, is tenure—the reward of a permanent job."

Poor teaching of English has a more tragic effect than any other kind, Fader believes, because he regards literacy as the basic tool for building a satisfactory life. No child can be educated in any subject, he points out in his book *Hooked on Books,* if that child "can't or won't read or write or listen well."

"Has anybody told you about all the desperate children, no longer children but unable to become adults, who inhabit the Job Corps camps?" he asks. "What do they want? A job, a trade, a way to buy a decent piece of the world they never made. . . . But how do you teach a boy to become a man who drives big rigs or repairs cars and trucks or cooks in a restaurant kitchen, if the boy can't read?"

This "poverty of experience," he adds—the poverty of a person limited to his own experience because he cannot read about the experiences of others—"can afflict lives lived at $100,000 a year just as readily as it curses the $1,000 a year existence."

Daniel Fader has developed a method for successfully teaching reading and writing to students whom English teachers have called "uneducable." And he has spent a great deal of time trying to convince those teachers to adopt it. He hasn't always spent the time willingly. "After all this isn't my business," he says. "My field is the Renaissance." But his deep anger over the number of "impoverished" children he has seen and known, and at the teaching profession which has allowed them to remain in their poverty, has driven him to do what he felt had to be done.

Fader first felt conscious concern about the problem of teaching children to read in 1961, the year he joined the University of Michigan faculty. Assigned the extracurricular task of serving as a University Accreditation Visitor, the tall handsome young professor drove around the state inspecting high schools with the purpose of rating their English programs.

He discovered that it wasn't easy to say whether a given school's program was good or bad. If he tried to rate it by the quality of students it turned out, he found himself in a dilemma.

Students planning to go on to college—the so-called "academic" students—generally seemed to do well in their English classes. This was true whether they went to a "highly recommended school" with others of their kind, or whether they represented a tiny minority in a school attended chiefly by "general" students, those not preparing or planning to go on to further formal education.

The general students, on the other hand, almost invariably did poorly. And again this was true whether they were part of a fairly homogeneous student body, or of one composed of both general and academic students. In the latter case, of course, the nonlearning general students were usually being taught by the very same teachers under whom academic students were doing well.

Fader was still puzzled by what he had seen when, one day, a Michigan education official asked him if he wouldn't like to write a program for teaching English in a school for delinquent boys. The school was a new Michigan state institution then in the process of construction.

"I was conned into accepting by the greatest of all lures—flattery," Fader remembered afterward. "I was reminded that since I had once been a delinquent myself, I would be able to understand how a delinquent's mind works."

The reference to his own past was to the fact that he had once spent his time, as he himself describes it, "shooting pool, gambling, fighting, staying out of school or breaking into it." And now that he had risen to the position of professor at an important university, the idea of recalling his own not-too-successful experiences with high school teaching techniques, and using them as a basis for an entirely different teaching approach, was irresistible. He agreed to prepare an English program that would be ready for the W. J. Maxey Boys' Training School when it opened. The school, named in honor of a man whose interest in youth had won him renown throughout Michigan, would be directed by that man's son, whom Fader knew to be equally devoted to young people. Fader was to be given a free hand. He set about preparing himself for the task.

First he again surveyed Michigan high schools, this time on his own. Over and over he asked English teachers why the nonlearners did not learn. Over and over he received the same answer: They did not learn because they did not want to; they were "educationally unaspiring" and therefore "essentially uneducable."

Why didn't they want to learn? Fader then asked.

To this question the teachers had no answer. It seemed to be a subject they had not thought about. As Fader later wrote, the "attitudes of readers and writers toward the processes of reading and writing have been regarded—when they have been considered at all—as no more important than the attitude of any mechanical object to the work it performs. Who would ask if a computer likes its work. . .?"

Fader decided he had been conducting the wrong survey. It was the students he needed to talk to, he told himself, not the teachers. Later he described what he learned during his subsequent conversations with dozens of them.

"What's wrong with your English class, I asked, that causes you to turn it off the way you do? You're out to lunch during your English class, I said, and I want to know why. They told me why: They told me it didn't make any difference about them. That the teacher didn't like them so they didn't like the teacher. She didn't talk about anything that mattered ('Sentence diagraming? Shoot! What do I care about that?') and she didn't talk like she *wanted* you to understand. And never nothing to read that was any good, even if you wanted to read. What difference does it make anyway?

"What difference does it make? The words are repeated so often that they become part of the litany with which the burial service for school is conducted. For the student not going on to college, school is dying and the English class is dead."

"What difference does it make?" That hopeless

question started a train of thought in Fader's mind that brought him up short.

Until that moment he had been assuming that the boys for whom he would be preparing an English program would be very much like the boy he himself had been. As he had thought ahead toward his program, he had been thinking back to what might have been helpful to a young Daniel Fader. ("Like so many other would-be innovators," he said afterward, "I looked more closely at myself than at my subjects.") But the young Daniel Fader, he suddenly realized, would never have asked, "What difference does it make?"

"When I was a kid I always talked about what I was going to do when I grew up," he says. "My friends did too. We thought there wasn't anything we couldn't be if we wanted to. We had confidence in the future. We had hope."

Now, looking again at his own past, but from a new point of view, he could see the reason for that hope. It helped him understand why these boys talked as they did.

Fader's parents were immigrants of little education who could give their children few material advantages. But they were determined that their children should have the education they had been denied, and one of the strict rules of their home was that Daniel must study in his room every day. If he "studied" books of his own choice rather than text books, he made sure they weren't aware of it.

Daniel's father couldn't bring his son and daughter

presents when he came home at night from his job as an insurance salesman, but he brought them something else. Every evening he arrived with a new word he had heard during the day. Often he could not spell it. Finding it in the dictionary became a game for the children and the aunts and uncles who always filled the Fader house in Baltimore.

"By the time we'd tracked the word down," Fader says, "it was a word none of us would ever forget."

Of his family he says, "It was always nice to come home every evening, because we always had such a good time together. A loving family," he adds, "is one of the two elements that can get anyone out of a ghetto. The other is having a lot of IQ points."

Fader had that second element too. By the time he was in high school he was bored with his teachers and what they were teaching him. He took to playing truant. He spent more time in Knocko's poolroom than he did in the classroom. But the poolroom didn't open until afternoon, and in any case he couldn't bring himself to let his parents know that he was avoiding the school by which they set such store. So he pretended to go to school by leaving home at eight o'clock in the morning, and "read away both morning and misery," as he puts it, at the Enoch Pratt Library.

As soon as he worked his way to the end of one shelf, he started on the next. At some point he read straight through the library's remarkable collection of eighteenth-century English periodicals, becoming so familiar with them that he would later be regarded as an authority on the subject.

160

A perceptive assistant high school principal found out where the truant Fader was spending his mornings. Somehow, Fader says, with this man's help, he got his high school diploma—and headed for Florida with the idea of earning his living playing pool.

It didn't work. "I was good," he says now, "but not that good."

And when he decided he wanted to go to college, there was a generous uncle in the background who offered help. At Cornell University Fader "majored" in philosophy and pool, winning both a BA degree and an intercollegiate billiards championship. After getting his master's degree at Cornell in 1954, he interrupted his studies with a stint in the United States Army Counterintelligence Corps. Two years in England followed, at Cambridge University, and then he took a Stanford University doctorate in English literature that led straight to his Michigan faculty post.

The differences between his young self and most of the kids Fader was now talking to in the Michigan schools were, he could see, far greater than the similarities. Few of them had either a loving family or "a lot of IQ points." They didn't believe in a rosy future because their past experiences had convinced them it didn't exist. Unlike their college-bound contemporaries, they were not willing to make present sacrifices—to struggle to absorb what an English teacher was trying to cram into their heads, for example—for the sake of future gratification in the shape of a college degree and the successful life it was said to lead to. For them that degree and that life belonged to a world they never expected to inhabit. Their environment had taught them, on the contrary, a live-for-today creed and a practicality that demanded a quick payoff for every effort.

Therefore, Fader concluded, they had two good reasons for not tuning in on their English classes. They saw no immediate payoff for any effort they might expend there, except in terms of a teacher's approval, which they didn't accept as coin of the realm. They saw no possibility of any future payoff at all.

Literacy to them, in other words, was a useless abstraction. Even a boy who could see some sense in math, or felt a flicker of interest in science or history, could see no point in what his English teacher was trying to teach him. It simply didn't seem to have anything to do with his life. And because he hated his English class, he also hated the reading and writing he was expected to do there—and consequently, inevitably, he did poorly in all his classes because he failed to master the basic techniques that would have enabled him to do otherwise.

His attitude toward his English teacher, moreover, affected those teachers in a way that resulted in further damage to him. Fader watched it happen in dozens of classrooms. He saw a teacher sparkle before a class of college-bound students, all eager for the good marks that were the open sesame to their bright future. Then he saw that same teacher turn into a grim jailer during the next hour when she faced sullen rows of boys and girls who stared past her, glassy-eyed. She didn't expect them to learn anything. She was resigned to the fact that she would "pass" them on, to get them out of school somehow, if they met her minimum requirement of orderly behavior. And they humored her by being silent in their passivity, in return for not having to struggle to learn.

In that vicious and hopeless circle "the bottom half of the young people . . . were being lost to public education," Fader decided. He was determined to break that circle.

". . . I knew there was no use identifying the children as causes of what was wrong in the English class," he wrote later. "They may be all that they shouldn't be, but they *are,* and must be met where they are before they can be led to where they *should* be (i.e., where *we* are).

"If not to the children—their lack of manners, their lack of interest, their deficient home environment etc., etc., etc." he asked, "then where to attribute the cause? Where else but to their teachers and the materials and methods they use?"

In what way could he change those elements, he then asked himself, to show young people of the "bottom half" that literacy can pay off not only economically but in terms of pleasure?

The program Fader finally devised for the Maxey Boys' Training School was based on the assumption that the chief requirement for learning reading and writing is not intellect, but motivation. It was a simple program, in theory at least, although it involved both new methods and new materials, and demanded new techniques and attitudes on the part of the teachers who would put it into practice. It consisted of two concepts which Fader called *saturation* and *diffusion.*

Fader explained both concepts to the teachers whom he interviewed for posts at the Maxey School. Both he and the school's director realized that the program would have no chance of working unless every member of the faculty understood it and was enthusiastic about it.

By saturation, Fader told them, he meant surrounding students with reading material chosen first to catch their eyes, then to meet their practical needs and match their interests. Among the materials he planned to use were magazines, newspapers, and brightly jacketed paperbound books totally unlike the drab hardbound texts and anthologies customary in English classes. His first goal was for the students to find joy in reading.

If a prospective teacher doubted that children could learn to write good English from such things, Fader answered that the important thing was for the students to learn to write with ease, and that it was better to write ungrammatically than not to be able to write at all.

To a prospective teacher who asked if a child should not be exposed to literature rather than to contemporary journalism, Fader answered that it was more practical for the child to read the newspaper. The paper was relevant to the child and therefore intrinsically interesting, Fader pointed out. He added that a newspaper might, as he put it, "prove to be the bridge across which he crawls, stumbles and finally walks erect, to where he should be"—and that a child might find Shakespeare at the other end of that bridge.

By diffusion, Fader explained, he meant spreading the responsibility for teaching reading and writing throughout the whole faculty. If a boy in a shop class wanted a wrench, Fader pointed out, the shop teacher would be expected to demand a written requisition for it. If a boy in an arithmetic class was solving problems about the speed of trains, the teacher would be expected to require him to write out at least some of those problems in words. Fader wanted each student to have at least two writing assignments each week in every class.

He put it this way: "No student is likely to learn to write if he believes that writing is an affliction visited upon defenseless students solely by English teachers." In other words he wanted practical-minded students, seeking an immediate payoff for their efforts, to realize that literacy was a must in all their classes. Once they realized that, Fader believed, they would learn those basic skills because, as he said, "Kids will do what they must to survive, including reading and writing."

The concept of diffusion gave Fader's program the name by which it would become known, "English in Every Classroom."

Fader also explained to his potential English teachers that he expected them to give their students a journal and require them to fill two pages of it every week. He did not expect the teachers to correct the journal, or even to read it. But he wanted the students to write and write and write, until writing became second nature to them. "Until that point is reached," Fader has explained, "practice will be far more beneficial to the student than correction."

Once he had selected a group of teachers who saw what he was driving at, and were eager to experiment along the lines he had laid down, Fader set to work with his English teachers to select the books to which the students would be exposed. He knew the boys at the school would be of junior high school age or older, but that most of them would have been classified as reading at no more than a fourth-grade level. He also knew that most of the boys, as he once wrote, "have lived materially disadvantaged lives; almost all have come from culturally impoverished worlds. At the age of twelve they know more about physical man—from sex of some kinds to violence of all kinds—than any child should and most adults ever will."

What kinds of books might such boys want to read? he and his teachers asked themselves. They drew up one list after another. They crossed off names and added new ones. And when they had completed a final list of 1,200 titles, Fader was afraid to spend the school's meager book budget on them for fear that many of the books would not appeal to the boys at all—and that he would then be left with no money to replace those mistakes with other materials.

He decided to seek help. In a letter to a commercial distributor of paperbacks and magazines, he wrote that he was making "a frank plea for charity, for without your help we are less likely to be able to teach literacy to those youthful criminals who are separated by language as well as action from the rest of society." He went on to say that the Maxey School could "make very good use of any paperbound book you carry which is likely to be read with pleasure by a boy from 12 to 17 years old," and offered to pay what he could toward the cost of the books "if you find our program deserving of your help.

"It is perhaps worth noting that if we are successful with these children," he concluded, "we will be opening an enormous untapped readership for publications such as those your company handles."

Two days after he had mailed off his letter he received a phone call from Ivan Ludington, head of the company Fader had written to. Ludington wanted to know exactly what Fader needed and offered to go to Ann Arbor to make arrangements for delivering a gift of books to the school. Fader, staggered at such generosity, insisted upon meeting Ludington in his Detroit office.

"Somehow that seemed to be the least I could do," Fader explained, writing about the experience some three years later. "It was also the most I could do. Since then, Mr. Ludington has been supplying the school . . . with all the paperbound books and magazines we request—absolutely free of any charge. Thus far the numbers are upwards of 10,000 paperbacks and 25,000 magazines."

When the Maxey School opened its doors in 1964, Fader made a point of being there as often as possible. It seemed likely to him that most of the newly arriving boys had never seen such a shining and well-scrubbed place set in such pleasantly landscaped grounds. He was sure none of them had ever seen anything like the school's library.

It had no shelves crowded with dull book spines bearing uninformative classification numbers. Instead it contained fourteen rotating steel racks, like the spinners used in bookshops, on which hundreds of books were displayed, all their vivid covers exposed. More books, also covers upward, along with magazines and newspapers, filled more racks along the walls. There were plenty of tables and plenty of chairs. There was no sign commanding silence.

"You may choose two books for your own," each boy was told by the librarian in attendance.

"You mean to keep?" the less shy boys asked.

"That's right," the librarian assured them. "To keep. You may take them to your room with you—take them anywhere you like. And if you finish them, and would like to trade them for another two, you may do that."

The titles the boys had to choose from were as various as the books' gay covers. They ranged from comic books through detective, suspense and horror stories, to sports stories, science fiction and war stories. There was nonfiction as well as fiction—self-help books, books about the facts of life, books on science and social action.

And when the boys moved off, books in their pockets, they found the textbooks in their classes were more paperbound books, or newspapers or magazines. Fader watched the boys in one room use a news magazine as their text; the students read various items from it and then plunged into a free-swinging talkfest that started with the evaluation of a new car and wound up with a discussion of new civil rights legislation. In other rooms he saw the sports section of the Detroit *News* (which contributed 100 newspapers a day to the school, or a chapter in Dick Gregory's book *Nigger,* set off similar lively talk.

He also saw the distaste with which the boys invariably reacted to the journals they were given in their English class. Their teacher's instruction—that each boy was to fill two of those empty pages each week, with anything he wanted to write—was frequently a signal for panic.

"What do you mean—anything?" some boy always asked.

"I mean just that," he was told. "Write anything at all. I won't even read it unless you ask me to. I just want you to fill the two pages."

The next question was predictable. "But suppose I can't think of anything?"

"Then copy something," the teacher told him, and Fader was not surprised at the answering gasps.

"The boys are always shocked and incredulous," Fader wrote once about this moment in every new boy's life. "In school, COPY is the dirtiest four-letter word they know. Punch your teacher in the nose. Break the windows and destroy the books. What can happen to you? Suspension? Probation? But whatever you do . . . *don't copy!*"

But at the Maxey School, under Fader's orders, boys were told to copy, if they liked—and many of them did at first. They copied pages of books and newspapers and magazines. One boy copied straight through a whole issue of *Time* magazine, always stopping at the end of his two pages even if he was in the middle of a sentence or a word.

Most of the boys, as Fader had anticipated, thought their journals represented a kind of novel and unusual punishment. To them writing was an agonizing chore. But because their laboriously written pages were never corrected, they gradually relaxed a little. The mere fact that they were not being constantly reinforced in their conviction that literacy was both unnecessary and beyond their grasp began to make a difference. In spite of themselves, as time went on, they found it easier to write those two pages. And almost invariably they finally got tired of copying and began to write something they had heard or thought or felt. Writing was becoming, for many of them, a tool they could use with some ease and confidence.

At the end of several months, Fader recalls, there was a noticeably different feel to the school. "We knew we had something going," he says, "but we didn't know exactly what it was."

Not long afterward he was able to tell an interviewer that they had "happy kids in a reform school"! Even to his own ears the statement sounded unlikely. He had always agreed with the usual dictum that "Nobody's got happy kids in a reform school."

But the boys at Maxey did seem happy, and there was overt evidence that the books with which they had been surrounded, not only in their library but in their classrooms and their living quarters, had something to do with it. They carried paperbound books with them wherever they went. Fader was aware that some of the boys still couldn't read the books sticking out of their back pockets, but they carried them just the same. At the Maxey School a book had become a status symbol, and it was a symbol available to all.

Furthermore, many of the boys who had said they couldn't read when they arrived at the school had been mysteriously transformed when they saw the reading material available to them. They might still spell out words haltingly and slowly, but they were reading. Some of them were reading books that most English teachers would have said were far beyond their level.

Fader recalls with special pleasure the student who took from the library display rack a copy of Nathaniel Hawthorne's *Scarlet Letter*. He explained that he'd heard it was about a whore, and that he wanted to read it even if his teacher did think it might be too hard for him.

"Three days later, on Monday," as Fader tells the story, "the same boy came to his English teacher with *The Scarlet Letter* in hand and two sheets of notebook paper. On those two sheets, front and back, were all the words—and their definitions—the boy hadn't known in the first eleven pages of the book. He had clearly spent the weekend with Hawthorne and the dictionary, and he was looking for praise—which he got, lavishly. His English teacher was amazed; the two sheets of notebook paper represented at least six hours of work. According to the teacher, this was a boy who may not have spent six hours reading since he was nine years old, and had no apparent idea of how to use a dictionary when he came to the Maxey School. . . . He produced no more lists, but he kept at the book (between other novels) for months; during that time, and long after, his conversations with his English teacher were full of his view of what was happening to Hester Prynne. . . . His valediction on Hawthorne's heroine may not have been couched in the author's own phrases, but it conveyed an understanding of the book that no one could improve upon: 'That woman,' he announced as he returned the book, 'she weren't no whore.' "

For Fader that incident reinforces his belief about the kinds of books that children can read with understanding, even if they don't know the meaning of every word.

"Semiliterate readers," he has written, "do not need semiliterate books. The simplistic language of much of the life-leeched literature inflicted upon the average schoolchild is not justifiable from any viewpoint. Bright, average, dull—however one classifies the child —he is immeasurably better off with books that are too difficult for him than books that are too simple. . . . In fact, the threshold of understanding . . . is surprisingly low, and even in many complex books can be pleasurably crossed by many simple readers."

In this connection Fader is quick to admit that of the 1,200 titles he and his staff originally chose for the school, 500 proved consistently popular; 700 remained almost unread. Those who had drawn up the list, Fader has said, including himself, would "never again have to be reminded of how little we know about the student we teach."

The Maxey staff had several means for discovering a book's true value to the boys. One was based on its "exchange value." Although the boys were permitted to return books they had read at any time, and trade them in for new ones, the supply of the most popular books was sometimes exhausted, and then copies of those books became a commodity for barter. Fader was not surprised when the James Bond books, war stories like *Run Silent, Run Deep* and *The Tunnel Escape,* and hot-rod stories such as *Road Rocket* and *Drag Strip* achieved the top going price of three cigarettes. But Fader was surprised as well as gratified to learn that three cigarettes were also demanded for copies of books by James Baldwin and Richard Wright, by John Steinbeck's *The Pearl,* Lorraine

Hansberry's *Raisin in the Sun* and—"the school's most widely read single title," as he once called it—John Howard Griffin's *Black Like Me*.

Of course the gradual emptying of the paperbound book display racks was another measure of the books' popularity. Once the racks became so bare that Fader and the school principal had to take unusual action. On a hot Saturday morning they held a "shakedown."

"Criminals' cells and delinquents' rooms have, in the history of penal institutions, been shaken down for everything from money and drugs, to knives, guns, files and blunt instruments," Fader wrote later, "but this may have been the first time they were shaken down for books. . . . We knew we'd find books, we never thought it would be like this. Books were everywhere: on their shelves, on their desks, their beds, their washstands. Their teachers said they were reading; the books they carried with them, stuffed in their pockets, said they were reading; the number of books missing from the library said they were reading . . . but here, suddenly, was evidence we couldn't question. It was a perversely happy two hours for both of us, faced as we were with the stolen evidence of our program's success."

But even that evidence, and the whole faculty's conviction that there were actually happy kids at the Maxey School, would not, Fader knew, convince the ordinary test-oriented public schoolteacher that his system of saturation and diffusion actually worked. That teacher would not believe it, Fader was convinced, unless she could be shown the kind of evidence she was accustomed to, in the form of charts and graphs and percentages tabulating test results.

Fader did not know of any existing tests that he could use to prove or disprove his point. He would not have been equipped to administer them if he had. He therefore needed two things: money and expert assistance.

For the first he applied to the United States Office of Education, and so effectively that he was granted $64,000 for the purpose of devising a program that would adequately test the results of English in Every Classroom. For the second he called on a Michigan University colleague, Dr. Elton B. McNeil of the university's psychology department.

McNeil later described their first encounter.

"I haven't got much time now,' I said to the man standing in the doorway of my office," McNeil wrote. "I didn't want to be rude to a colleague—even if he was from the English Department—but the fact was that I *didn't* have much time. After an hour and a half of the time I didn't have, I watched him leave my office and I realized I'd been had by an expert. I was hooked on *English in Every Classroom.*

"Dan Fader is a former poolroom hustler who cares as much about kids as a child psychologist, which he isn't, and as much about language as a Renaissance scholar, which he is," McNeil added. "He's also one of the greatest idea-pushers of our time. Brushing aside my objections as though he hadn't heard them —and he probably hadn't—he pursued me from one excuse to another. . . . By the time he left my office I had agreed to test his thesis. Without Fader, the idea is persuasive. With him, it's irresistible."

McNeil had spent a good many years working "in clinical and educational settings," as he put it, "with socially and culturally deprived children." And at first he "found it difficult to believe that anything so simple as Fader's idea could make a significant difference in their behavior."

Nevertheless, he and the staff he gathered together worked out a series of tests unlike any tests children had ever been given before. Then they gave the tests to the boys at the Maxey School and to a control group of boys of similar age and background in another Michigan state training school for delinquents. The boys in the control group were different from the Maxey School boys in only one important way: They were not exposed to Fader's methods.

Some of the tests in the program measured the boys' attitudes—how they felt about themselves and about school and the things they were required to do there. The results showed that the boys in the control group worried more about their schoolwork after being in their training school for a year than they had when they arrived there, and that during that year their attitude toward themselves—their self-esteem—had fallen. But the boys at the Maxey School had lost some of their anxiety about schoolwork during that year, and felt better about themselves at the end of it; their self-esteem had increased.

Other tests in the program measured actual literacy

achievement, or lack of it. Results showed that the Maxey School boys' verbal proficiency, their ability to perform with words and ideas, noticeably increased after they had been exposed to Fader's methods for a year.

In that particular "race with only two entries," McNeil wrote later, "our control group did worse than run second—it finished farther back than its own starting point." While the Maxey School boys had "performed so well," he pointed out, "the boys in our control sample were unable even to maintain their unsatisfactory level of the year before. . . ."

Dr. McNeil concluded, "Though the results are as we hoped they would be, they are nonetheless shocking, for they are impersonal reflections of the fate of living human beings exposed to a crippling educational and social environment. . . . Given intellectual deprivation in an overworked and understaffed institution, we can hardly expect pupils to hold their own in the battle for verbal survival."

The test results bore out the opinion Fader had formed when he was visiting public schools before he planned his English in Every Classroom program. There too he had seen children sliding backward in "a crippling educational and social environment." He was therefore convinced that his program could work as effectively in public schools as in penal institutions. And he was glad, however jealous he was of the time required, to respond to the queries from public school officials that had already been reaching him from every part of the country.

One such query came from officials of the badly overcrowded Garnet-Patterson Junior High School in Washington, D.C., an institution which drew a large part of its student body from underprivileged homes. They wanted to introduce English in Every Classroom into their school and asked Fader to come to Washington to install his program. He agreed. In the fall of 1965 Garnet-Patterson Junior High School became the first public school to follow Fader's methods.

That same year Ivan Ludington asked Fader how long it would take to introduce English in Every Classroom into every school in Detroit, and in Wayne County.

Fader, thinking of the usual attitudes of educators, replied, "If you're speaking of curriculum change, it may take forever."

But Ludington was less ambitious. He had in mind the setting up in school buildings of reading rooms stocked with paperbound books and magazines—rooms like the colorful Maxey School library furnished with rotating racks and open shelves and tables and chairs. He wondered if the schools would set aside space for such reading rooms, provided he contributed the reading materials.

Fader said he didn't know.

Ludington said, "Let's find out," and invited groups of teachers and school officials to be his guests at lunch to discuss his plan. Fader attended each of the fifteen luncheon meetings Ludington arranged, and outlined the program used at the Maxey School. Ludington then made his offer of free materials to any school willing to accept them.

By no means were all the initial reactions favorable. Teachers and school officials often openly resented the man they sometimes spoke of as the "so-called expert from a university." They often resented Ludington too, because they felt sure there must be some ulterior motive lurking behind his offer. But eventually all the schools but one agreed to Ludington's plan, and new reading rooms began to open up. One was in Detroit's huge Northwestern High School.

"In the first ten days of its operation," Fader reported afterward, "over 1,500 of the school's 2,700 students visited the room and 1,850 books were put into circulation." He added, since he realized those early figures might be taken as proof of nothing but enthusiasm for novelty, that nine months later: "In nine September school days, 1,147 students visited the reading room and left with more than 1,000 books."

As the news began to spread about students in Washington and Detroit schools who were suddenly showing increased ability to read and write, Fader was invited to appear all over the country to address interested groups. Often he had Ludington's help in meeting his traveling expenses. He talked to teachers and school officials. He talked to distributors of books, magazines and newspapers, urging the kind of cooperation between them and school authorities which had made the Ludington Reading Rooms possible.

At the same time Fader, with the assistance of University of Michigan psychologist Dr. Morton H. Shaevitz, wrote the first edition of *Hooked on Books*, which expanded an earlier pamphlet Fader had prepared on his program. Soon the paperbound book was selling widely, and a second edition appeared. This one included a report, prepared by McNeil, on the testing program which had been devised and first tried out on the boys of the Maxey School and on their control in another similar institution.

Other less scientifically compiled data were also beginning to appear, bolstering McNeil's belief that "Fader's educational theory is as sound as his pool game." Within a few years after Fader devised his teaching methods, they were achieving good results in schools in some forty states and three foreign countries. At the Kilmer Job Corps Center in New Jersey they were turning school dropouts into readers. In Detroit, Police Commissioner Ray Girardin was crediting the new school reading rooms with reducing the city's juvenile delinquency rate.

"Fader's program is a fine idea," the commissioner told a reporter from the *Michigan Daily*. "It is a real help to us and we plan to cooperate any way we can."

Fader himself hesitated to agree that the reading rooms were directly responsible for a decrease in delinquency. But his faith in books and reading was too deep for him to rule out the possibility, especially because he knew many parents had joined their children in those rooms, or read the books their children had brought home.

"Is it possible," he has asked, "that kids who read in a community where reading is valued, where adults are eager to read the same books and magazines, become kids who have lost their most compelling reason —the frustration and alienation of pure, unbearable boredom—for breaking the law?"

Now, with his methods already well known, Fader readily says they are no panacea for all the ills of present-day education. He does feel that the English in Every Classroom program can help break down "compartmentalized education" built on "a theory which declares each man sufficient unto his subject and each subject sufficient unto itself." It can help each teacher in an educational system profit from his co-workers, he believes, rather than remain "so concerned with protecting his feudal rights."

Fader says, however, that his methods can achieve only what good teachers have always achieved: the stimulation of a child to develop himself to the utmost of his ability. What he chiefly regrets today is the lack of enough good teachers who are ready to do their best for dull children as well as bright ones, for black children as well as white.

He does feel that the situation is improving. He talks with enthusiasm of the many highly motivated, well-educated and intelligent young teachers, both black and white, both men and women, now appearing on school faculties. He applauds the higher teachers' salaries that have drawn many of them—particularly men with families to support—into the field.

Those salaries, he feels, are not only of economic importance to teachers and potential teachers. They are also important as reflecting the growing concern of the community for education.

"When a community becomes education-oriented," he says, "its citizens will demand real education from their school systems. And then the public schools will provide that kind of education for everyone."

In the meantime, although he has officially returned to his own field of the Renaissance, Daniel Fader, father of two children of his own, goes on prodding educators to teach all children not only to read and write, but to find pleasure in those skills. And if at times his goal of every child being "hooked on books" seems distant, he recalls the remark a Maxey School delinquent made to him on the day of the book shakedown.

"Like reading, man," the boy said. "You know—it ain't so bad."

6

Protectors of the Unborn

FRANCES KELSEY & HELEN TAUSSIG

Frances Oldham Kelsey, M.D., started work as a medical officer with the Food and Drug Administration in August, 1960, processing applications for new-drug approvals without which "new" drugs may not be sold in the United States. The first NDA, or New Drug Application, assigned to her came from the William S. Merrell Company; it sought approval of Kevadon, a sleeping pill already being widely marketed in Europe under other trade names. Kevadon's active ingredient was the drug thalidomide.

Though Dr. Kelsey had no way of knowing it at the time, thalidomide had already been responsible for the birth of hideously deformed babies in West Germany, where the drug had been sold for some three years. Even German doctors had not yet learned the cause of those tragic births which eventually numbered in the thousands throughout Europe. That thousands of similarly deformed babies were not born in the United States was owing almost entirely to Dr. Kelsey —the stubborn Dr. Kelsey, as she was often called—and to Dr. Helen B. Taussig of Johns Hopkins University Hospital who played an important role in the final chapter of the amazing story of thalidomide in America.

Dr. Kelsey was an experienced physician and pharmacologist when she joined the FDA. Born Frances Oldham in 1914, on Vancouver Island in British Columbia, she had majored in science at Montreal's McGill University. A fellowship brought her to the United States to take her doctor's degree at the University of Chicago and then to join that university's faculty as a pharmacologist. A few years later she married another Chicago University pharmacologist, F. Ellis Kelsey, and left her job because the university did not permit husband and wife to teach in the same department. During the next four years she gave birth to two daughters, Susan and Christine, and took her medical degree.

In 1952, when her husband was named head of the Department of Physiology and Pharmacology at the University of South Dakota's School of Medicine, the Kelsey family moved to Vermillion, South Dakota. There, after completing her internship, Frances joined the School of Medicine's faculty for three years as an associate professor of medicine. During that period she and her husband organized several courses specially designed for the practicing physicians of the state. Afterward she practiced medicine in Vermillion, and frequently took over the practice of a doctor in some small isolated one-doctor community, when that physician was ill or had to be away. Her tall spare figure, her face that seemed a little severe until she smiled, became known in more than half a dozen South Dakota counties.

In 1960 the Kelseys moved to a suburb of Washington, D.C. Dr. Ellis Kelsey had been called to the National Institutes of Health, the research institutions of the Public Health Service. Like the Food and Drug Administration, these institutes are a part of the Department of Health, Education, and Welfare. Frances' background ensured her a welcome at the FDA's Bureau of Medicine.

In a drab uncarpeted office, in what had once been a barracks erected during a wartime space emergency, Dr. Frances Kelsey settled to work on her initial assignment, Merrell's NDA for Kevadon. The application filled several large volumes of charts, figures, and reports, each as thick as a big-city telephone directory. They dealt with Kevadon's chemistry, with the pharmacological and clinical studies that had been done on the drug, and with the marketing description and labeling Merrell intended to use on its new product.

Dr. Kelsey's responsibility was to evaluate Kevadon for its safety. (Before the passage of new legislation in 1962 the FDA had no authority to demand proof of a drug's effectiveness for its intended uses.) She handed some of the volumes to the bureau's chemists and pharmacologists, and tackled the rest herself, reading and rereading hundreds of pages of words and figures. Bureau regulations required that an NDA had to be accepted within sixty days of its submission, or be declared unacceptable within that time; in the latter case it could be resubmitted in a revised form if the applying company wished.

Merrell took for granted that the report on Kevadon would be favorable. Thalidomide had been used since 1957 in West Germany where its originator—from whom Merrell had obtained a license to manufacture and distribute the drug in the United States and Canada—sold it under the trade name of Contergan. In England it was already selling as Distaval. In Portugal it was being distributed as Softenon. And everywhere it had been hailed as the best sedative ever devised. Throughout Europe thalidomide sleeping pills were selling by the millions, in some cases over the druggist's counter, without prescription.

European reports on thalidomide, alone or in combination with other drugs, seemed consistently enthusiastic. (Not until years later, when the German originator of the drug was being sued by hundreds of parents of deformed children, did the public learn that contrary reports had been repressed.) All insomniacs who took thalidomide were said to awake in the morning refreshed and with no drug hangover. Sufferers from asthma and neuralgia took it to relieve pain and discomfort. It calmed children when they were irritable. (Dr. Taussig once described it as "West Germany's baby sitter.") It counteracted nausea in pregnant women. Even a heavy overdose was said to have proved harmless, and one manufacturer's ad emphasized its safety by showing a child taking a bottle of thalidomide pills from a shelf.

In October, 1960, therefore, only a few weeks after submitting its New Drug Application to the FDA, the 134-year-old Merrell company, experienced in the techniques of drug promotion, inaugurated a Kevadon Hospital Clinical Program. It called together its corps of detail men, who are to the drug industry what traveling salesmen are to other manufacturers, and gave them instructions on how to invite doctors to undertake "experiments" with Kevadon. At that time the law permitted such experimental programs to be carried out without the surveillance of the FDA; investigating doctors did not even have to tell patients that they were being used as guinea pigs.

"We have firmly established the safety, dosage and usefulness of Kevadon by both foreign and U.S. laboratory and clinical studies," the manual issued to the detail men stated. "This program is designed to gain widespread *confirmation* of its usefulness in a variety of hospitalized patients. If your work yields case reports, personal communications or published work, all well and good. But the main purpose is to establish local studies whose results will be spread among hospital staff members. You can assure your

187

doctors that they need not report results if they don't want to but that we, naturally, would like to know of their results. . . .

"At the beginning of your interview, don't be secretive—lay your cards on the table," the manual added. "Tell the doctor that present plans call for Kevadon to be marketed early in 1961. Let them know the basic clinical research on Kevadon has been done. . . . *Appeal to the doctor's ego—we think he is important enough to be selected as one of the first to use Kevadon in that section of the country."*

Merrell was setting the stage for the sale of what it expected to be a highly profitable new product.

Its investigational program succeeded even beyond its expectations. Merrell had hoped that 750 "studies" of Kevadon, involving some 15,000 patients, would be set up by the end of November. By mid-November it was sending its detailmen airmail special-delivery letters with the message "Cease Fire—You Made It." The men had, Merrell said, "exceeded the 'quota' for the number of studies and doubled the 'quota' for the number of patients."

But by then Merrell had already received Dr. Kelsey's report on its NDA. On November 10, just before the sixty-day period ran out, she had informed the company that its application was incomplete and inadequate to demonstrate the drug's safety. She specifically described the chemical data as incomplete, and the proposed labeling as "unsuitable."

Merrell automatically resubmitted its application, and in the next two months Dr. Kelsey received four new batches of data on the drug. Once she had a personal visit from Merrell's director of scientific relations, Dr. F. Joseph Murray, who some weeks earlier had made it his business to learn who was handling his company's NDA. And as the second sixty-day period drew to an end, in January, 1961, Dr. Murray wrote her asking to be informed immediately by telephone if the application was now acceptable. He reminded her that Merrell was eager to proceed with plans for its promised "early in 1961" marketing date.

Dr. Kelsey's response was a second official communication stating that the Kevadon NDA was unacceptable. She had shown the Merrell material to her pharmacologist husband at the National Institutes— the various divisions of the HEW Department frequently confer with one another—and the resulting memo, from Dr. F. E. Kelsey to Dr. F. O. Kelsey, had confirmed her own opinion. Her husband had written that one section of the NDA was "an interesting collection of meaningless pseudoscientific jargon apparently intended to impress chemically unsophisticated readers." Of another section he had written, "I cannot believe this to be honest incompetence."

By then Kevadon was no longer Dr. Kelsey's sole concern. She had been assigned other work, and she had also become involved in time-consuming hearings on the drug Altafur, which the FDA had approved in July, 1959, but had found unsafe by December, 1960, and was trying to remove from the market. Its order to halt the drug's sale had been appealed by the manufacturer, and Altafur remained available to the public while the appeal was heard. FDA staff members were understandably eager to bring the hearing to a speedy and satisfactory end, and to see removed from sale a drug which some of them felt had been too hastily approved in the first place.

Consequently, when Dr. Murray tried to reach Dr. Kelsey by phone a week after the Merrell NDA was turned down for the second time, and again resubmitted, he found her unavailable. He therefore called Dr. Ralph G. Smith, director of the FDA's New Drug Division and Dr. Kelsey's superior. Dr. Murray assured Dr. Smith that Merrell's application was being held up now only because the revised labeling suggested by the company had not yet been reviewed. He hoped for its early aproval. Dr. Smith promised to check into the matter.

A week later Dr. Murray called Dr. Smith again, and was told that Dr. Smith had discussed the subject with Dr. Kelsey and learned that considerable material, in addition to the new labeling, remained to be reviewed. Dr. Murray mentioned Merrell's disrupted marketing schedule, and asked to be called if there was anything he could do to hurry the application along.

On the first of February Dr. Murray reached Dr. Kelsey by phone. He told her Kevadon was now scheduled for release March 6, and that Merrell wanted to begin to print its labeling. Dr. Kelsey made no promise of an early approval.

In the next two weeks there were more phone calls.

Dr. Murray admitted he was under pressure from his company to get the NDA approved, and said the Merrell vice-president wanted to come to Washington to see what he could do about hastening the process.

By this time Dr. Kelsey knew she was being a thorn in Merrell's side. The realization gave her no pleasure. She was not trying to wage a vendetta against the drug manufacturer. As a doctor and a pharmacologist she had long been aware of the value of many of the new drugs that had been produced by industry-financed research. At the University of South Dakota she had been the three-year recipient of a Medical Faculty Award from one of the country's leading drug manufacturers. Her own relations with the manufacturers, in other words, had been what she called "usually amiable."

"We see their point of view and they see ours," she said. Then she added, "But the responsibility for releasing a drug is ours, not theirs."

In the matter of Kevadon she had taken that responsibility with characteristic seriousness from the beginning. She had always felt, as she put it, that there was "something peculiar" about thalidomide. It did not put animals to sleep, for example, although it was such an effective sedative for human beings. This made her wonder whether animals and humans might not react differently to the drug on other levels as well—whether, in fact, animal tests of the drug should be accepted as proving its safety for humans.

Another matter troubled Dr. Kelsey too. During

the war years, while studying quinine in connection with a malaria project, she had proved that a fetus does not always react to a chemical substance in the same way an adult does. "The fetus or newborn may be, pharmacologically, an entirely different organism from the adult," she once explained. For that reason she was not convinced that thalidomide was harmless to a fetus, even though it seemed harmless for adults. And she had consequently requested, from the outset, information to show that the use of thaildomide was safe during pregnancy.

As time went by, Merrell's pressures on her became heavier. Phone call followed phone call; visit followed visit. Each made her more acutely aware than before that Merrell regarded her as "a bureaucratic nit picker," as someone once put it.

And then one day late in February, while reading through copies of the *British Medical Journal,* Dr. Kelsey came across an interesting letter to the editor in the December 31, 1960, issue. It was headed "Is Thalidomide to Blame?"

The letter had been written by an Aberdeenshire doctor who wished to know if any fellow physicians had shared his experience: Four of his patients, who had been taking thalidomide for from eighteen month to two years, had developed peripheral neuritis (a tingling numbness of hands and feet) and occasional lack of muscular coordination. He had stopped administering the drug, he wrote, and after a few months three of the patients showed a marked improvement. The fourth patient had stopped taking the drug too recently to be evaluated.

"It would appear that these symptoms could possibly be a toxic effect of thalidomide," the doctor concluded. "I have seen no record of similar effects with this drug, and I feel it would be of interest to learn whether any of your readers may have observed these effects after long-term treatment with the drug."

Dr. Kelsey was more than interested. She was definitely disturbed.

"If this drug were a cancer treatment, or helpful in really dread diseases," she said afterward, explaining her attitude, "I wouldn't have worried about minor side effects."

But it wasn't. It was a sleeping pill—one more sleeping pill to be added to an already long list of available and satisfactory sedatives.

"And I could anticipate the results of an enthusiastic sales effort," Dr. Kelsey added. "Everybody—sick and well, old and young—would be taking it. That's why . . . I felt I couldn't be too careful."

She promptly wrote to the Merrell Company, describing the letter she had just read and asking for further data on animal studies and clinical information. She also asked for a list of the doctors to whom the drug had been given for investigation.

And when Dr. Murray called her that same day, "to inquire about Kevadon," she told him what she had just put in her letter.

Recalling that day a few years later, when she was

testifying before a Senate subcommittee about her part in the thalidomide story, Dr. Kelsey said of the Merrell staff scientists, "They said they too had read the article, and they did not consider this was very significant, as many older persons did get peripheral neuritis, and they felt it was just a chance association."

To Dr. Kelsey the finding had seemed so crucial that she did not feel she should have been left to discover it for herself by the chance perusal of a magazine. She subsequently wrote the company a letter stating that she felt its representatives had not been completely frank with her, by not volunteering the information that they too had read that *British Medical Journal* item. Dr. Murray told Dr. Smith he considered Dr. Kelsey's letter "somewhat libelous," and Dr. Kelsey was concerned enough to consult a lawyer. Otherwise she tried to ignore this new example of industry pressure.

In the meantime, since Dr. Kelsey required further data on the possible toxicity of Kevadon, Dr. Murray went to England. On his return he reported to Dr. Kelsey on his findings there, and on comments from some of Merrell's American investigators. He admitted that neurological symptoms did occur with prolonged use of Kevadon, but declared that if discovered in time, the effects were apparently reversible.

Dr. Kelsey repeated her conviction that she and her associates regarded the toxicity of Kevadon as serious.

In that same month of March, Dr. Murray and Merrell's medical director visited the FDA office to submit some further data and to urgently request that their application be approved with the condition that they include "precautionary information" on the drug's label, warning doctors of what they still claimed was the very slight possibility of Kevadon's toxicity.

Dr. Kelsey replied that the material on Kevadon required further review. And on the last day of March her letter went out once again to Merrell, declaring its application for the third time, in the official phrase, "considered withdrawn and resubmitted."

On April 5 further data was given to her, with a letter which pointed out how long Kevadon had been under review, and stating Merrell's conviction that the data now in Dr. Kelsey's hands was adequate to support approval. The letter also said Merrell was concerned to know of Dr. Kelsey's plan to make a study of thalidomide and related drugs—a plan which Merrell obviously feared would cause further delay. The letter concluded with a request that the decision on Kevadon be telephoned to Merrell as soon as possible.

On April 19—with Kevadon already approved in Canada and on sale there—Dr. Murray called Dr. Smith and told the director of the New Drug Division that Merrell felt "some pressure should be exerted." It wanted "a 'Yes' or 'No' decision," so that the company could prepare to go to a hearing if necessary. It "believed Dr. Kelsey was avoiding a decision." The vice-president of Merrell planned to call on the FDA Commissioner himself "if nothing was going to be done."

That time Dr. Kelsey did not wait for the end of

a sixty-day period. On May 5 a letter went out to Merrell once more declaring its application "incomplete and inadequate." Dr. Kelsey wanted still more animal studies and more clinical information, in order to evaluate "the seriousness of neurological toxicity."

She had received, in the meantime, in response to her request for the names of the doctor investigators of Kevadon, a list of fifty-six names. These physicians, Merrell explained, had used the drug for more than four months prior to her February request. The company did not inform her that Kevadon was also in the hands of hundreds of other doctors, who had been told that "they need not report results if they don't want to."

In correspondence with one of the doctors whose names she had been given, Dr. Kelsey wrote that she agreed with his statement to her that peripheral neuritis seemed to be the only side effect thalidomide caused. But she added that the FDA was not satisfied that the effect was always completely reversible, and that it might occur more frequently than the doctor himself seemed to believe.

The phone calls and visits from Merrell representatives continued. And though more data reached Dr. Kelsey's office, it was never enough to satisfy her. On July 26 she sent out her fifth letter stating that the Kevadon NDA was "regarded as withdrawn and resubmitted."

On September 7, at Merrell's urging, a conference of company representatives and clinical investigators met with Dr. Kelsey and several other FDA staff members, including Dr. Smith. A Bureau of Medicine memo on the conference reported: "The investigators presented their experience with Kevadon. This included evidence that the drug is effective, has certain advantages over other hypnotics regarding safety, does cause neurological reactions, and some evidence but not conclusive evidence that the reactions are necessarily reversible. There was only a little evidence that the drug would be harmless to the fetus if given during pregnancy, and this evidence was not adequate."

Less than a week later Dr. Kelsey's sixth letter went out declaring the application for Kevadon unacceptable.

Dr. Kelsey did not have to guess what its reception would be. Of the 125 NDA's for human drugs her office had received during that year, 23 had been approved within sixty days and 90 by the end of eight months. Now a year had gone by since she had first received Merrell's application, and she had still not given it her approval. She was not surprised that the people at Merrell were angry. But she felt there was nothing else she could do.

Merrell soon proposed new and more cautious labeling. Dr. Kelsey wanted more data.

Dr. Murray telephoned her, and Dr. Smith as well, urging them to predict when the NDA might be finally accepted. He said Merrell now hoped to get the drug on the market by the middle of November—ten long months past its original target date. Neither Dr. Smith nor Dr. Kelsey could give him an optimistic answer.

And on November 7, for the seventh time, Dr. Kelsey reported Merrell's application unacceptable.

Three weeks later a shaken Dr. Murray telephoned her the news he had just received in a cablegram from Europe: Thalidomide was being withdrawn from the West German market because of reports that it was associated—Dr. Murray hastened to state that he hoped the association would prove merely coincidental—with certain congenital deformities.

The news of those deformities and their suspected cause had burst like a bombshell on the West German public. The skillful medical detective work that lay behind it had begun well over two years before, in 1959.

That year thirteen West German babies had been born with the malformation known as phocomelia. The name, from the Greek for "seal" and "limb," is starkly descriptive: A baby with phocomelia has tiny flippers instead of arms and hands. Flippers may also replace the feet and legs.

Until 1959 cases of phocomelia were so rare that one elderly German doctor said he had seen as many two-headed babies during his career as babies afflicted with this deformity. And, until that year, most cases showed deformity in only one limb. But in 1959 many infants were born in whom all four limbs were deformed. And the phocomelia cases appeared more and more frequently. University pediatric clinics alone reported 124 of them in West Germany during 1960.

In that year, too, the first phocomelia babies were born in England. Some died at birth or soon afterward. They were perhaps the lucky ones, Dr. Taussig has said. But two out of three survived.

German doctors had been desperately seeking the cause of the deformities from the beginning. Heredity did not seem to be involved, although in earlier cases phocomelia had often been traced back through a family.

The doctors concluded, as Dr. Taussig wrote later in one of the first American articles on the subject, that "an unknown agent from the environment, affecting the embryo at some time between the third and sixth week of pregnancy, had caused the damage. During this period, when most women do not yet know they are pregnant, the embryo goes through the principal stages of development."

But what was that agent? An infection of German measles, during the critical period of gestation, had long been recognized as a possible cause of malformed embryos, but those malformations were not the ones of phocomelia. Any other virus cause seemed equally unlikely, in fact, because the cases of phocomelia increased steadily in number but were in the beginning all confined to West Germany. Dozens of possible causes were considered and discarded, including radioactive fallout.

One doctor active in the search, the distinguished Widukind Lenz of Hamburg, sent out questionnaires to parents of deformed babies and to their physicians.

He asked them to report on each mother's diet during pregnancy, and on a variety of things she might have been exposed to during that period, such as household detergents, drugs and hormones, X rays, contraceptive devices and pregnancy tests. When he correlated their replies, he learned, among other things, that 20 percent of the mothers had taken thalidomide under its German trade name, Contergan.

Twenty was not a very high percentage, Dr. Lenz realized, but he was aware that many women might have forgotten to report the taking of so common a drug. He immediately queried all the mothers again, asking specifically about Contergan. This time half reported having taken it.

On November 15, 1961—a week after Dr. Kelsey had sent out her seventh not-approved letter to Merrell— Dr. Lenz reported to the German manufacturer of Contergan that he believed it might be responsible for the sudden widespread incidence of phocomelia, and asked the company to withdraw the drug from the market.

Five days later he told a meeting of pediatricians that he believed he had traced the cause of phocomelia to a commonly used drug—he did not name it—and that he had asked the manufacturer to cease its sale. Afterward one of the doctors present came up to him and asked, "Will you tell me, confidentially, is the drug Contergan? I ask because we have such a child and my wife took Contergan." Before that meeting was over, all the doctors attending it knew that the reputable Dr. Lenz believed Contergan was causing the deformed births throughout the country.

On November 26, Contergan was withdrawn from the German market, along with all compounds containing thalidomide. Forty-eight hours later the Ministry of Health of West Germany warned the public that Contergan was the suspected cause of phocomelia. Newspapers and radio and television stations joined in urging women not to take the drug.

At almost exactly the same time a similar medical deduction had been made in Australia by Dr. W. G. McBride, who had for some time been interested in the possible adverse effects of drugs taken during pregnancy. When Dr. McBride saw three newly born babies with phocomelia in April, 1961, he had studied their mothers' histories and discovered that all three women had taken thalidomide—sold in Australia under its British trade name, Distaval—early in their pregnancies. In October and November he investigated three additional cases of phocomelia; in those cases too the three mothers involved had taken Distaval during early pregnancy. Dr. McBride promptly notified the manufacturers of the drug of his findings and conclusions. His report, reaching England simultaneously with the news from Germany, caused the British manufacturer of Distaval to remove it from the market.

Dr. Murray had made his November 30 phone call to Dr. Kelsey as soon as he heard the news from Germany. But Merrell felt that the case against thalidomide was not yet proved. So, apparently, did George P. Larrick, then Commissioner of the Food and Drug Administration, and a man generally regarded as friendly to the drug industry and sympathetic to its problems. At any event he did not take matters into his own hands—as he had the power to do—and order the rounding up of all the Kevadon that had been distributed to American doctors. Instead he left the matter to Merrell's discretion.

On December 4 Merrell's medical director, Dr. John N. Premi, sent out a warning letter which read:

DEAR DOCTOR:

We have received information from abroad on the occurrence of congenital malformations in the offspring of a few mothers who had taken thalidomide (marketed in Canada as Kevadon) early in their pregnancies. It is impossible at this time to determine whether, in fact, there is any causal relationship.

However, until definitive information is available to us, as a precaution we are adding the following contraindication to the use of Kevadon:

Kevadon should not be administered to pregnant women nor to premenopausal women who may become pregnant.

We are actively following this matter and you will be advised when it is finally determined whether or not this precautionary step was necessary.

The FDA staff learned only later that that letter had gone to none but the doctors who had received supplies of Kevadon during the past twelve months. These numbered only some 10 percent of all the doctors who had received the drug, inasmuch as Merrell's big Kevadon Hospital Clinical Program had been inaugurated, and exceeded its "quota," more than a year before.

Three weeks later Dr. Kelsey sent out her eighth and last letter declaring the Kevadon NDA incomplete "in the absence of data relative to the deformities of newborn babies." That time Merrell did not resubmit its application.

Kevadon was not going to be marketed in the United States. That fact was now assured, and Dr. Kelsey was responsible for it.

But hundreds of doctors throughout the country still had Merrell's donated supplies of Kevadon on hand, and neither they nor their patients had been warned against its use. The drug thalidomide and its danger were still totally unknown to the general American public.

"One of the striking things to me," Dr. Taussig has said, "was that there was very widespread publicity in Germany in November, 1961, and scarcely a word of it reached our press over here."

No word at all had reached the American press by January, 1962, when Dr. Helen Taussig entered the story.

Most famous as codeveloper of the blue baby operation, which has saved the lives of so many infants, Dr. Taussig had been associated with the Johns Hopkins University School of Medicine ever since she took her medical degree there in 1925. She was professor of pediatrics at Johns Hopkins University in 1959 (she became professor emeritus in 1963). Her reputation as a pediatric cardiologist was worldwide. Awards and honorary degrees had been bestowed on her on three continents during her long and distinguished career.

On an evening in January, 1962, Dr. Taussig was visited, as she so often was, by one of the many foreign doctors who had earlier studied under her at Johns Hopkins. Dr. Alois Beuren of West Germany had returned to the United States for a short time; he was flying home the following morning. It was he who gave Dr. Taussig her first news of thalidomide.

"He told me," Dr. Taussig later explained, "that the doctors in West Germany were seeing a great number of children born with gross malformations of the extremities, little flippers instead of arms or legs, or no arms or no legs; and what was more, that Dr. Lenz thought the malformation was caused by a sleeping tablet."

By the next morning Dr. Taussig realized, as she has said, "the full implication of the situation, namely, the danger which might lurk in drugs if indeed it were true that a sleeping tablet did cause such a malformation." She promptly made up her mind that she wanted to see those deformed babies for herself, and talk to the doctors who had studied them. An airmail letter to Dr. Beuren brought the immediately telephoned reply that she would be welcomed as an investigator in West Germany.

Three weeks later, after arranging for her absence from Johns Hopkins, and fulfilling various commitments she could not cancel, Dr. Taussig flew to Hamburg.

The chief of the Kinder Klinic where Dr. Beuren worked lent her his hospital's best resident to guide her on a round of flying visits to other hospitals and pediatric clinics throughout West Germany.

What she saw horrified her. What she heard made her realize how difficult it had been to trace the association between thalidomide and birth deformities—an association that some German doctors still doubted. From Dr. Lenz she learned that out of one group of 100 women who had taken the drug during pregnancy, only 2 had given birth to deformed babies. To many people this might have seemed small reason to indict thalidomide. Dr. Lenz, who knew the times at which these two women had taken thalidomide, realized that only those 2 women had taken the drug during the brief period when it might cause deformities in the developing fetus. Therefore this report was a serious indictment indeed.

Some of the incidents he related to her she found particularly conclusive. One had to do with a mother whose baby was deformed, but whose doctor swore she had not received Contergan. The doctor had prescribed, he insisted, an entirely different sedative. But when Dr. Lenz checked the records of the pharmacy that had filled the prescription, he found it stamped by the druggist: "Drug not in stock. Contergan given instead."

Dr. Taussig made a brief study stop in England before she returned to Baltimore. "I had left Germany 90 percent convinced that thalidomide was the responsible factor," she said later. "I left England 99 percent convinced."

Before she returned home, *Time* magazine, in its February 23 issue, had published an article entitled "Sleeping Pill Nightmare." It might have appeared earlier. The magazine's West German correspondent had alerted his New York office to the Contergan scare the previous November. Nothing had been done about it then, since thalidomide under the name of Contergan was unknown in the United States, and *Time's* editors believed the news would have no interest for American readers. (The whole thalidomide story has since been pointed to as an example of the need for labeling all drugs by their generic, or scientific, name, as well as by their brand name.) But when *Time's* medical editor realized that thalidomide was the basic ingredient of Kevadon, already being sold in Canada and offered for consideration to the United States Food and Drug Administration, he hurried the article into print.

It related the history of Contergan and its association with European birth deformities. Then it said that all Canadian doctors had been warned against the use of Kevadon the previous December, and that the drug had been used only "under heavy restrictions" in the United States where "the cautious Food and Drug Administration confined Kevadon to medical researchers 'for investigational use only.' " Consequently, the article concluded, American consumption had "been small—though some American women travelers have brought foreign pills home in their pocketbooks."

The article also stated—inaccurately, as events proved—that "U.S. investigators using the drug received a warning similar to that sent to Canadian doctors."

Dr. Taussig was back in Baltimore by April 1. There she learned that Dr. John O. Nestor, medical officer of the FDA and another of her former students, had tried to reach her while she was away. When he had been told the reason for her absence, he had left an urgent message asking her to get in touch with him on her return.

She telephoned Dr. Nestor, and within a matter of days he and Dr. Kelsey visited her at Johns Hopkins.

Dr. Kelsey's memorandum of their visit says, "Such information as I had received prior to Dr. Taussig's report was to the effect that the association between the drug and the malformations was perhaps not wholly established particularly in view of the fact that the drug had been used for several years in Europe before any difficulty arose. Dr. Taussig said this was simply not true."

She and Dr. Taussig were in instant agreement that

the American public must be warned without delay about the dangers of thalidomide. The warning must be issued, they felt, even if it protected only a single baby born to a woman who might have brought thalidomide pills home with her from Europe, or who might have been given such pills by one of Merrell's investigating doctors.

Dr. Taussig offered to do anything in her power to help the FDA protect possible sufferers from Kevadon. But Dr. Kelsey did not have the authority to accept her offer, and it was not accepted by the Food and Drug Administration itself.

Since there was therefore no way in which the two women doctors could officially coordinate their efforts, each carried on the campaign in her own way.

Dr. Kelsey asked Merrell to send her a "complete and up-to-date list of all physicians supplied with the drug," and information on what the company had done to warn those doctors against its use. When she received the list, she was appalled to discover that it contained a total of 1,267 names.

Dr. Kelsey then realized, for the first time, that only a small number of the investigating doctors had received the warning letter which Merrell had sent out in December, 1961. All the doctors had, however, been sent a letter from Merrell in March, 1962 (after the *Time* article appeared), asking them to cease further investigation of the drug, and to destroy or return all the Kevadon they still possessed. But when

Dr. Kelsey read a copy of that letter, she was not reassured.

In spite of the fact that Dr. Lenz had, as she put it, presented "overwhelming evidence to support his belief that thalidomide is teratogenic [deforming] to man," the letter stated that from Merrell's investigations to date, "no causal relationship between thalidomide and teratogenic effects has been established."

Dr. Kelsey informed her superiors about what she regarded as the inadequate urgency of the letter, but the FDA hierarchy still made no move on its own. It continued to leave the situation in Merrell's hands, and as later appeared, Merrell's records of the amount of Kevadon returned or destroyed were alarmingly vague.

Dr. Taussig, in the meantime, had written a brief editorial on her German experience and requested the American Medical Association to publish it immediately in its *Journal,* probably the most widely read of American medical publications. The editors refused. They stated that *Time* magazine had already reported on the possible danger of thalidomide.

The AMA *Journal* did publish an article by her on thalidomide in June, but before it appeared she had addressed medical meetings at every opportunity. As soon as possible after her April 1 return she had made a report on thalidomide to Johns Hopkins Hospital and to the University of Maryland. Two weeks later she spoke before the American College of Physicians in Philadelphia, and two weeks after that to the

American Pediatric Society. Late in May she was asked to testify before a subcommittee of the Judiciary Committee on Food and Drug Regulations. She agreed, provided she were permitted to show the committee members some pictures.

After presenting to them several photographs of babies deformed by phocomelia, she said, "I may not be a pharmacologist, or even a great physiologist, but I am sure that if any of you had a child or a grandchild with such malformations, you would be doing everything in your power to prevent it happening again, and that is why I am here today."

Dr. Taussig's article in the AMA *Journal* appeared June 30. Another article she had written for *Scientific American,* a magazine with a broader circulation, was ready for publication in August. But in the meantime Dr. Kelsey had been interviewed by three reporters. One got the up-to-date facts on thalidomide but decided to hold her story for a while. ("She could have kicked herself afterward," Dr. Kelsey recalled later.) The other two were from Washington newspapers, one from the *Star,* the other from the *Post.*

It was the experienced science reporter Morton Mintz of the *Post* who finally gave thalidomide the great splash of publicity that both Dr. Kelsey and Dr. Taussig had hoped for. His report, headlined "HEROINE" OF FDA KEEPS BAD DRUGS OFF MARKET, and illustrated with a photograph of Dr. Kelsey, landed on the *Post*'s July 15 front page and was picked up by the wire services for distribution all over the country.

"This is the story," it began, "of how the skepticism

and stubbornness of a Government physician prevented what could have been an appalling American tragedy, the birth of hundreds, of indeed thousands of armless and legless children."

Suddenly the whole nation was thalidomide-conscious. The question immediately arose of whether doctors and hospitals or their patients still had any of the drug on hand. Not all the distributed Kevadon pills had been labeled. The possibility thus had to be faced that some people might still be given, or have in their possession, pills which they did not know to be thalidomide and which they might unwittingly take.

For the first time the FDA looked into Merrell's records and found that the company could not account for all the Kevadon it had distributed. FDA field-workers were put on the job, to check up on every investigating doctor individually.

On August 1 Dr. Kelsey and FDA Commissioner Larrick were testifying before a Senate subcommittee which was hearing evidence on the need for new drug legislation. Commissioner Larrick was sharply questioned about why the FDA itself had not ordered the drug withdrawn as soon as the German evidence of phocomelia became known. He said he had felt it unnecessary because Merrell had carried out that role "with reasonable diligence." Then he was forced to admit that "in spite of the fact that they tried very hard, we have, within the last few days, still found some of the drug. . . ."

Five days later, on August 6, President John Kennedy publicly appealed to all Americans to clear out of their medicine cabinets, and destroy, all unidentified pills.

On August 23 a report on the FDA's "search and destroy" mission revealed that a total of over 2,500,000 thalidomide pills, and "lesser quantities of liquids and powders containing the drug," had been distributed by Merrell. The FDA itself had recovered more than 25,000 unlabeled pills from 79 physicians, and by then had interviewed 1,168 of the 1,267 investigating doctors—some of whom had moved since receiving the drug, and others of whom had died.

"More than 50 percent had no record of the quantities returned or destroyed," the report said.

Most of the doctors said they had received Merrell's March letter advising them to stop using the drug, but 42 claimed they had been given no such warning.

In spite of everything Dr. Kelsey and Dr. Taussig had been able to do, some deformed babies were born in the United States. In ten cases, proof existed that the mothers had been given the drug by their doctor or hospital, and taken it during those critical early weeks of pregnancy. In seven other cases the mothers were known to have obtained thalidomide abroad. In the remaining nine cases no proof could be established that the mother had taken thalidomide at the critical time. One woman, who knew she had taken it early in her pregnancy, tried to obtain an abortion on that ground, but was unable to do so in the United States.

She flew to Sweden, where she was aborted of a deformed fetus.

The thalidomide story is credited with having rescued from oblivion the so-called Kefauver-Harris Drug Amendments, which had apparently been permanently buried only a few weeks before the story broke. Shortly after the whole country had been aroused by that story, the amendments were passed. Since 1962, therefore, the public has been protected by various new regulations. One of them gives the FDA stronger controls over such investigational procedures as Merrell's Kevadon Hospital Clinical Program. Now, for example, when a doctor gives a patient a new and still-unapproved drug, as part of an investigatory program, he must tell the patient that he is doing so.

The thalidomide story has also been credited with spurring a more determined study of the possible effects of all drugs on the fetus. And it has given rise to warnings which may have saved immeasurable suffering. Dr. Taussig repeated one of them at every opportunity: "Woman of childbearing age should avoid drugs as much as possible, particularly new ones."

Her role in the thalidomide story added to her already wide renown. In 1964 the Medal of Freedom, bestowed on her by President Lyndon Johnson, was added to the long list of awards she had already received.

The President's Award for Distinguished Federal

213

Civilian Service came earlier to Dr. Kelsey, who would soon be named director of the FDA's Division of Scientific Investigations. It was given to her by President Kennedy in 1962. Senator Kefauver, who proposed her for it, wrote the President that "her contribution flows from a rare combination of factors: a knowledge of medicine, a knowledge of pharmacology, a keen intellect, an inquiring mind, the imagination to connect apparently isolated bits of information, and the strength of character to resist strong pressures."

Neither of the two doctors had done what they did in the hope of winning awards. Dr. Kelsey's pleasure in her medal from the President's hand was perhaps no greater than her delight in a tiny scrap of rug, barely big enough to rest both feet on, given to her by her colleagues after they had read newspaper accounts of the FDA heroine's uncarpeted office.

Dr. Kelsey and Dr. Taussig did what they did because they knew that—as Edmond Cahn wrote in his *Drugs in Our Society*—"So many did not really care, did not even want to know what the new drugs might cost in terms of human injuries and fatalities."

Dr. Taussig and Dr. Kelsey did care. They did want to know. They went on caring and wanting to know when the dramatic story of thalidomide had ended.

"The worst did not happen," Dr. Kelsey said matter-of-factly then. "Now let's go on and see what we can learn."

7

Protagonist of a Free Theater

JOSEPH PAPP

"Don't tell me anything is impossible. Let's try it first," Joseph Papp frequently says. He said it to the friend who declared Papp's idea of giving New Yorkers a free Shakespearean theater was "completely impossible." Then Papp tried it. With no fortune of his own to draw on, and no rich or powerful friends, with no assets at all except talent, the ability to persuade others to his point of view, and a dogged refusal to accept the dictum that you can't fight city hall, Joseph Papp set out to give his hometown what he wanted it to have. Today there is scarcely a New Yorker who does not know that he succeeded, and who has not had reason to thank him for the New York Shakespeare Festival.

Joseph Papp was born in 1921, son of a trunkmaker

and a seamstress. His boyhood coincided with the years of the 1930's depression. He spent it in the Williamsburg section of Brooklyn, one of the toughest neighborhoods of New York, where the streets were battlefields for young gang fighters.

"There used to be Jewish gangs—I came from a family of Polish Jews—and Italian gangs and colored gangs in our neighborhood," he remembers. "The colored gangs outnumbered the others, so my gang used to team up with the Italians in street fights."

One day, when he was about thirteen, something happened to him. He remembers that too.

"I was standing on a street corner watching one of the neighbors punch another guy in the face," he says, "and it suddenly came over me that there must be something better than fighting. I started to change from that point. I began taking books out of the library, and I discovered Shakespeare."

After that Papp worked nights in a laundry in order to stay in high school. He became interested in dramatics. He found he had a knack for memorizing long speeches, and he enjoyed reciting them. Slight, dark and intense, he looked, as a critic would say later, "something like a turn-of-the-century tragedian." He began to dream of a career in the theater.

After a few years of odd jobs, and a four-year stretch in the World War II Navy, he used his GI Bill to study acting and directing for two years at the Actors Laboratory Theatre in Hollywood. There were two further years of apprenticeship in New York before he landed his first real job. Doubling as understudy and assistant stage manager, he went out with a Broadway touring company playing Arthur Miller's *Death of a Salesman*. The next year, 1951, he produced and directed plays with a small professional company at a New York State lake resort.

During the tour of *Death of a Salesman* Papp had met Peggy Marie Bennion, who had been a reporter for a Salt Lake City newspaper before she turned actress for a time. They were maried late in 1951 and settled down in New York. Papp applied for work at the New York studios of CBS-TV and was hired as a stage manager, assigned to one of the popular panel shows. He was also given the opportunity to do several of the plays produced by the network's famous *Studio One*. If any of his old Williamsburg gang ran into him in those days, they must have felt that Joe Papp had made it, and on his own terms.

But Joe Papp didn't think he belonged in the world in which he had succeeded. He was spending his free time seeking some place in the theater where he would really feel at home.

"That's what everybody wants, isn't it?" he asks. "A place of your own—a home."

He sought it first in the existing noncommercial theater. He worked with the Equity Library Theater, sponsored by New York's professional actors' union to give nonworking actors a chance to practice their profession. With a cast that included his wife, who would soon give up acting for psychiatric social work, he directed three one-act plays by Sean O'Casey at one of the early manifestations of what was to become the Off-Broadway theater. He used Negroes in his cast and generally approached the O'Casey works untraditionally. Brooks Atkinson, influential critic of the New York *Times* and devoted admirer of the Irish playwright, was horrified by the Papp-directed performances. Joseph Papp, he wrote, should get out of the theater.

But another reputable New York critic declared that Papp's work was the best he had seen that year. Papp made up his mind to organize his own workshop group in order to experiment freely with the plays he had always most wanted to do—those of Shakespeare, Marlowe, Kyd and other Elizabethans.

His first requirement was physical space. He found it in an unused basement of the Emmanuel Presbyterian Church on New York's Lower East Side, where newly arrived Puerto Rican immigrants were rapidly replacing older residents. The Reverend Clarence Boyer, good-naturedly doubtful of the value of Papp's project, nevertheless welcomed the embryonic theater as a community activity of his church. Papp's group thus became one of the first of many church-sponsored little theaters in the city.

There were no seats and no stage in the big bare basement room. Lack of a stage didn't trouble Papp. Working "on the flat" simply presented a particular kind of directorial challenge. Lack of seats was a real problem. On one of the first scrounging forays that would soon absorb so much of his time and energy, Papp found 150 old ones free for the taking in a decrepit Bronx movie house. He also found a CBS technician willing to help him acquire them.

Together they crawled around the theater's concrete floor for two days, removing the chairs by chiseling off the rusted bolts that held each one in place. They transported them to Manhattan in a borrowed truck. They bolted them down again in their own "theater." But the first time an actor sat on one of the seats, he toppled over backward: The floorboards of the church basement were so rotten that the bolts had ripped out. So the two amateur carpenters had to spend a further two days in the shallow crawl space beneath the floor, wet handkerchiefs over their faces to keep out the choking dust, screwing metal reinforcing plates to the soft wood. Then they unbolted all the chairs and bolted them down once more.

"Even then you had to sit just so in those seats," Papp recalls now. "We hadn't known much about what we were doing, and we didn't get all the plates in exactly the right place."

He had also been given some of the Bronx theater's lighting equipment, and was almost electrocuted trying to remove it. Nobody had warned him that the current in the old movie house was still turned on.

Papp's own money, some $75 of it, paid for many of the materials necessary for putting his workshop theater into usable condition. The owner of a neighborhood Army-Navy surplus store, where much of that equipment was obtained, earned the title of Papp's financial associate by contributing a similar sum to the new young enterprise.

Many people in the world of the theater, professional and would-be professional, were eager to join Papp's group. Some of them, working in television or on Broadway, saw his plan as an opportunity to try out ideas of their own with which they had never had a chance to experiment. Others belonged to what Papp called the city's "dispossessed actors," that large number of young people unable to find roles in the profit-oriented commercial theater because of its notorious reluctance to risk hiring unknowns.

Together, in the basement room that could never be adequately heated by an ancient furnace, they all talked and argued and read scenes from Elizabethan drama. Papp urgently desired to serve as the group's director. He had his own definite ideas of how to present the centuries-old plays in such a way that they would be moving and credible to a modern audience. But he was willing to subordinate himself to others, not only to actors but to directors as well, in order to hold the group together until it could become a viable unit.

"I was willing to do all the manual labor, all the dirtiest jobs," he says, "if we could just create a real theater."

Not everyone who joined the group stayed with it. "The thing would get competitive," Papp says, "and people would leave. Or they would leave because they didn't find the rest of us congenial. You have to work with people who are compatible if you're really going to create something. So anyone who joined us for a couple of evenings, and found he wasn't happy there, just naturally didn't come back."

Stuart Vaughan was one brilliant director who stayed, because he and Papp found they agreed on basic principles. Among others who did not leave, or left only to return at the first opportunity, were a number of young actors and actresses who would soon become widely known, including Colleen Dewhurst, Paul Stevens, George C. Scott, and Briarly Lee. A number of CBS technicians stayed too, and were generous about covering for Papp at CBS when his presence was urgently required at the Wooden O, as their makeshift theater had been christened.

The group's first performance open to the public consisted of several individual scenes staged by various directors and casts. A few brief sentences in the mimeographed Emmanuel Church bulletin had announced the event, stating that no admission would be charged but that voluntary donations—to be divided equally between the workshop and the church—would be welcome. Most of the members of the audience who came on that and subsequent evenings arrived by taxi from uptown. They were friends and co-workers of workshop members, curious about this newest of the many small theater groups in the city.

"On nights when all our seats were occupied, we sometimes took in as much as sixty dollars," Papp remembers.

Soon he was producing *As You Like It* on a regular

two-nights-a-week basis, and matinees of *Two Gentlemen of Verona*. Most of the players in the latter were working actors not free to appear evenings at the church.

As You Like It was done in modern dress, partly to save costume costs, but chiefly to conform to the philosophy which was gradually shaping the workshop into a distinctive unit. That philosophy had developed out of Papp's desire "to achieve modernity without sacrificing the form and poetry of Shakespeare, and without vulgarizing the period," as he put it. He wanted his stage to be "free of bombast and conventional stage artifices." He sought "gutsy" actors who could project the reality of Twentieth-century movies and television.

"There is a definite kind of reality in today's movie and TV acting, however superficial it may be," Papp has said. "It is the kind of acting we are all most accustomed to: It belongs to our generation. That's what we wanted and that's what we tried to achieve."

The first critic who visited the Wooden O, in late October of 1955, was Frances Herridge of the New York *Post*. The next day she devoted her whole column to it. She assured her readers that they owed themselves the pleasure of an evening with the Shakespearean Theater Workshop, and that they could have it without standing in line at a box office or ordering expensive tickets ahead of time. She urged them to telephone first to make sure seats were available—she gave them the workshop's number—and then simply to go and enjoy themselves.

After that more critics came. Meyer Levin, the novelist who reviewed plays for an important suburban paper, wrote that Papp's company gave "some of the most skillful and talented performances of the season."

Before the year's end Papp's workshop had joined the ranks of producing groups taken seriously by the regular theatergoing public. He was pleased with the respect the group had won from such a discriminating audience. He was dissatisfied because his theater played no part in the life of the community. Papp had even experimented with a play in Spanish, which he had tried to cast partly with neighborhood Puerto Rican women. They had been briefly curious. They had attended a rehearsal or two. Then they had disappeared. And almost no local residents attended workshop performances.

"The theater just wasn't their place," Papp says. "They didn't feel at home there."

He could understand why that was so. The theater was no more a part of their lives, he realized, than it had been a part of the ghetto life of his own early boyhood. His East Side neighbors relished entertainment. They watched television and went to the movies. But it would simply never have occurred to them to go uptown to a Broadway theater, even if they could have afforded the price of a ticket. To them the theater was part of another and totally alien world.

Papp had hoped that a free theater would break the pattern of their theaterless lives. He had even

223

believed that a free theater could make regular theatergoers of them, just as a free library had once made a regular reader out of him, and that they would eventually buy theater tickets if they were able to do so, just as early library users like himself began to buy books whenever they could.

Papp's strong social conscience furthermore insisted that people were as entitled to a free theater as to free libraries. His hope of providing one for a small group of people had not worked. His theater's neighbors remained what he thought of as a "dispossessed audience," deprived—as seriously deprived as actors lacking an audience—because they had missed the horizon-stretching experience which in Papp's opinion only the living theater could provide.

Wondering how he could bring together this dispossessed audience and the dispossessed actors of his workship, he finally decided that if the members of the audience would not enter a theater, he must take his theater out of doors into the neighborhood with which they were already familiar.

He had already taken what would prove to be an important step in his new plan. Equipped, as he once put it, with "no influence, no pull, no nuthin', just talk," he had obtained a charter from the New York State Department of Education. The department authorities had previously issued charters only to museums and other demonstrably educational institutions. Papp, convinced that his theater also qualified as an educational body, had wanted the charter for the status it would confer on his workshop, and, just as important, because it would permit him to seek contributions on a tax-deductible basis.

Now he persuaded municipal officials to give him the use, for the following summer, of a city-owned open-air amphitheater on the shore of Manhattan's East River, until then utilized only occasionally for concerts and dance recitals. Its tiers of seats rose above a concrete stage 40 yards deep and 44 yards across, complete with dressing rooms, lights and other necessities. It lay close to the water's edge between the looming towers of the Williamsburg and Manhattan bridges.

In the early summer of 1956 Papp and Vaughan began rehearsing *Julius Caesar* on that stage. Papp was launching what one critic would call "a shoestring operation so audacious as to seem almost ludicrous." He had a capital of just $200 contributed by sympathetic friends. His actors and crew, having obtained special permission from their unions, were working for nothing but carfare. Whatever other expenses arose, Papp assumed he would meet somehow, out of his own pocket if necessary. The problem that really concerned him was producing a play that would be meaningful to the people he hoped would see it.

He watched the children who gathered around the edge of the stage when the rehearsals were under way—neighborhood youngsters curious about the strange grown-ups striding across the vast concrete stage. The children stared and listened and giggled. Soon they were aping the actors. "Hail, Caesar!" boys shouted to one another with upraised arms, and Papp grinned.

He grinned again when the contagion affected Park Department workers readying the stage for its new use. "Brutus, where goest thou?" one called as noon approached. "Lean Cassius, I go to grab my lunch," another workman answered.

These reactions from their impromptu audience convinced Papp that he had been right when he insisted, as he often had, that there would be a special excitement in playing Shakespeare for people to whom it would be as fresh as if it had just been written. "Imagine doing *Romeo and Juliet*," he had told his group, "for people who think the two kids are actually going to get married and live happily ever after!"

Midway through rehearsals Papp realized that some of the youthful members of his cast were unable to project their voices to the farthest rows of the big amphitheater. He needed an amplifier, which he knew would cost $500. Just as he was—"begrimed, unshaven and unslept," he described himself later— he headed for the New York office of ANTA, the American National Theatre and Academy.

"You've got to put up the money for our amplifier!" he announced when he walked in.

"They just stared at me, all those ladies," he recalled afterward, "but they gave me five hundred dollars."

His *Julius Caesar* was scheduled to open on the evening of June 20. But as the date approached, Papp lacked enough money to rent all the costumes, props and other equipment he needed. He postponed the opening until June 29 and spent a frantic week writing begging letters and making begging telephone calls. He acquired $5 here and $10 there, until he had enough to pay his rental fees for a few days. By the late afternoon of June 29 everything was at hand.

Papp and the members of his company had invited their friends and various influential people in the theater and the city administration to be present that night. They reminded themselves that if none of those guests showed up, they might play to an empty house.

But early that evening people began to pour into the theater. They came by ones, by twos, by dozens. There were children among them, including some who had watched the rehearsals. There were teenagers, young parents with babies in their arms, and old men and women. Long before curtaintime they filled every space in the 2,000-seat theater. And as the minutes ticked by, they grew restless and impatient. "Hurry it up!" some of them shouted. "What are you waiting for?"

Papp was faced with the kind of audience he had always dreamed of, and he was terrified.

"It sounded like Ebbets Field during a pregame warm-up," he told somebody afterward. "Frankly, I was scared to death. I didn't have the faintest notion of what to expect. Obviously most of those people out there had never even seen live actors before. They might stone us to death, for all I knew."

At last the lights went up. The play began.

"They became absolutely still," Papp said afterward. "Too still, I thought. Not a sound, right through Marullus' tirade against the mob for honoring Caesar and forgetting Pompey. You know? 'You blocks, you stones, you worse than senseless things!' At the end of the speech a great cheer went up—the kind you hear when Gil Hodges hits in the clutch. Here was an audience that really *identified*. I've never felt so relieved in my life."

As the actor swept on through the play, the people in the audience followed every twist of the plot with intent interest. They gasped when Caesar's assassins raised their daggers and killed him. They cheered Antony's speech which turned the Roman crowd against Caesar's enemies. They applauded the end of every long speech and every scene. They cheered and applauded when warring armies brought the play to a close.

No one present that night doubted that Papp had triumphed. He and his dispossessed actors had brought Shakespeare to a dispossessed audience, and the audience had loved it.

Meyer Berger, unofficial chronicler of the city in his New York *Times* column, wrote that that production of *Julius Caesar* "worked a minor miracle." He described in particular the "special thrill" of the moment when Caesar had said, "But I am constant as the northern star," and pointed to the heavens. The audience had followed the actor's upward glance and together they all had seen the actual northern star shining high above the stage as if, Berger wrote, "even night's vault had been recruited for the scene."

Variety, the theater world's newspaper, headlined its report of the play's opening with typical irreverence but unmistakable approval: NY PARK CAESAR HAS OK PREEM. New York City critics raved.

Two weeks later Papp was $750 in debt for rental fees. A *Times* reporter heard the news and printed it, along with Papp's statement that the three weekly performances of what he was calling the New York Summer Shakespeare Festival would cease unless the bills could somehow be paid.

Herman Levin, the Broadway producer whose *My Fair Lady* was then playing to packed houses, telephoned Papp within hours after the paper appeared. "I read that you need seven hundred and fifty dollars," Levin said. "Is that all?"

Papp said that amount would enable him to keep going.

"Come over to my office and pick up the check," Levin told him.

Other friendly donations trickled in to make up the total of $2,000 which Papp spent that season on his *Julius Caesar* and *The Taming of the Shrew*.

Before the summer ended, Papp even had the public approval of Brooks Atkinson, who had once announced that the young Joseph Papp should leave the theater. Papp had called at Atkinson's office in a truck, the only vehicle he was able to borrow at the moment, waited for hours until he could speak to the *Times* critic, and finally convinced Atkinson to attend that night's performance. In the following Sunday's paper Atkinson made handsome amends for his earlier harsh words with an enthusiastic review of the Papp production. The thousands of New Yorkers who took Atkinson's word for gospel promptly followed his advice and went to see the Shakespeare being enacted on the banks of the East River.

"I told Atkinson later, when we became good friends," Papp says, "that he was responsible for both the worst and the best thing that ever happened to me."

By autumn, when the group returned to its East Side church home, Papp was already planning a far more ambitious schedule for the next summer. He figured it would cost $30,000.

Part of that sum he planned to invest in a mobile stage, a modern version of the pageant wagons that once carried companies of traveling players from one English town to another. A friend from his Williamsburg gang fighting days, who had become a machine shop proprietor, located a secondhand trailer truck. Together they devised a stage that could be folded up to form the van's sides, with enough space inside to hold painted backdrops and a balcony for Juliet. The mechanic did the job for what it cost him. Papp had his mobile stage for $3,000.

In the meantime he was visiting, telephoning and writing to dozens of city officials, trying to obtain permission to stage his plays the following summer at various municipal parksites. He was determined to bring Shakespeare not only to Manhattan again, but also to each of the other four boroughs of New York City: Brooklyn, Bronx, Queens and Staten Island.

Six long months went by before he was able to convince the right people that his project deserved municipal assistance. Then, at last, he received the permits he needed and other help as well. The city gave him the use of 2,000 folding chairs, the services of a handful of Park Department employees, and the promise of police protection.

By early spring of 1957 Papp's plans were well along. He had chosen the three plays he would present during the summer: *Romeo and Juliet, Two Gentlemen of Verona,* and *Macbeth.* He had rounded up a staff willing to work with him for nothing, or next to nothing. Among them was his much-praised director, Stuart Vaughan, an electrician, a stage manager, a set designer, a choreographer, a fencing instructor, a wardrobe mistress and a press agent. David Amram, then a rising young composer, was providing him with original recorded background music for his plays, performed by volunteer professional musicians with the help of volunteer professional sound technicians. Papp was also negotiating for the loan of lighting and amplifying equipment.

Some of his cast and stage crew were volunteer apprentices, working for nothing. "Presumably," a friendly reporter wrote later, they kept themselves alive during the summer "by foraging for roots and berries in the parks.' But Papp meant to pay the Equity minimum salary, then $40 a week, to those of his actors who belonged to Equity, and lesser salaries to some of the others. He therefore had to post a bond with Equity before he opend.

He needed money.

By March he had a pledge of $10,000 from the Doris

Duke Foundation, and the promise of another $10,000 from the New York Foundation, dependent on his raising $5,000 on his own first. By April he was still $1,600 short of that goal, but small donations were still coming in. They were undoubtedly encouraged by a citation Papp received just then from the national American Shakespeare Festival and Academy, for an "outstanding Shakespearean contribution."

In May, on the greensward of Manhattan's Central Park, on the shore of a lake and against the effective background of the park's Belvedere Tower, he opened his summer season—still lacking his full $30,000. He delighted his audiences and pleased the critics. Then he packed up his props and took his mobile stage out into New York's other boroughs.

His stage crew, composed chiefly of what he called "nice young lads and eager as hell," lacked muscle and experience. All the equipment was heavy. It included two 35-foot steel towers for supporting loudspeakers and lights. The young apprentices worked eighteen hours every time they set up or took down the stage— and longer when breakdowns occurred.

"Our equipment began to come apart right off the bat," Papp recalled afterward.

In July, at the end of three weeks of performances, he reluctantly abandoned his mobile stage—he later sold it—and his traveling productions. He announced that for the rest of the summer he would present all festival performances in Central Park.

A sympathetic press reported his change of plans

and urged members of the public to support Papp's theater. They did, though mostly with small sums. Before the first performance of *Macbeth,* Papp announced that he would have to close the play after opening night for lack of funds. But he borrowed the money and kept the play going.

In the meantime "Shakespeare in the Park," as New Yorkers were calling it, was becoming a fixture of the city's summer life. People arrived early, to make sure of their first-come-first-served seats. They picnicked while they waited for the play to begin, on sandwiches out of paper bags or cold chicken and champagne from elaborate hampers. They read; they talked. Children ran up and down the aisles. Thousands of New Yorkers got acquainted with one another in a new way during those hours of twilight before the lights went up, silence fell, and the first actors walked out onto the stage.

City officials, who had previously worried about the increasing amount of crime in the park, were pleased that the crowd of 2,000 people pouring into the area each evening transformed it, as one columnist declared, "from a threatening jungle into a tranquil place for healthy entertainment."

"You have made the park lovely again," one grateful New Yorker wrote Joseph Papp.

Resolved to take advantage of the overwhelming success of his first summer of free Shakespeare in New York, Papp began to seek indoor quarters where free Shakespeare might continue through the winter. His first choice was a theater that existed under the protective umbrella of the City of New York. He found the Heckscher Theater buried away in the Welfare Department's Children's Center on the upper reaches of Fifth Avenue at 104th Street. Mayor Robert Wagner responded to his urgent pleas by making it available to him for a first season of winter Shakespeare.

The Heckscher would give Papp a properly equipped indoor stage for the first time. Its location also had many advantages over that of the Emmanuel Church, which was two long bus trips each way from the homes of many of his actors, some of whom—like himself—worked daytimes to support wives and families. At about the same time Howard Cullman, well-known civic leader, agreed to head a fund-raising drive for Papp's company.

Papp opened at the Heckscher in November with *Richard III*. It ran there until January. In the meantime he had won what he regarded as another important victory. After badgering the authorities for months, he had been granted permission to present Shakespeare in the city's schools, in particular to students in the poorer neighborhoods. His Shakespeare Festival, in other words, had been officially incorporated into the city's educational system. Students would attend the plays as extensions of their English courses.

The school program proved successful from the start.

"TV is full of tricks, but you feel as if this was really happening," one fourteen-year-old commented.

"It was so exciting I never realized they were speaking Shakespeare," another wrote.

Unprompted by their teachers, students sometimes passed the hat during their after-performance discussions in English class, and made their own contributions of nickels and dimes to the Shakespeare Festival. They wrote editorials in their school newspapers urging its support.

In January, 1958, Papp was ready to follow his Heckscher production of *Richard III* with *As You Like It*. But by then the fund-raising drive on behalf of the festival had produced only enough to keep that play open for a week of previews, which Papp had already promised to audiences from New York's youth and welfare organizations. He therefore planned to seek a grant of $40,000 from the city Board of Estimate, to finance the rest of the season. He believed his festival had sufficiently established itself as a part of the city's cultural life to be deserving of municipal support. He could tell the board, for example, that 18,000 people had already mailed in requests for tickets to *As You Like It*.

Actors Equity was only one of the strong voices raised in defense of Papp's appeal. None of them was strong enough. The appeal was rejected.

The press, solidly behind Papp as it had been from the start, deplored the decision. "William Shakespeare has some disillusioning things to say about politicians, even statesmen," a New York *Times* editorial began, "and doubtless these days Joseph Papp, one of this city's most successful producers of Shakespeare, unhappily concurs. So might New York. . . ." New York might especially feel so, the *Times* added, since the city appropriated $50,000 a year for free concerts in the parks, and the mayor had just recently urged his fellow citizens not to neglect "the social studies and the humanities, the basic strength of our civilization."

One reporter pointed out that the Shakespeare Festival had recently been featured on the cover of *Amerika,* the U.S. government's Russian-language publication prepared for distribution in the Soviet Union. The magazine had called the festival an example of "the free popular culture in our country." Could America now let Papp down so soon after thus making use of him for its own propaganda purposes? the reporter was in effect asking his public.

Many of Papp's staunchest friends thought the festival, whose existence had always been so precarious, was now doomed. Papp told reporters, "I've dedicated my life to this and I don't mean to stop now." He gave them an urgent message for the public: "Write letters. Send money. Please."

The public responded. People wrote letters by the hundreds to city officials and to newspapers. One declared indignantly that it was "disgraceful and incredible that the largest city in the world should officially decline to support an invaluable dramatic offering like the Shakespeare Festival."

Actors Equity gave the festival $1,500. Individuals sent money too. During the week of previews of *As*

You Like It some $1,400 arrived, mostly in small amounts. One check for $100 came from a former municipal employee who wrote that he was sending it because he knew how hard it was to get money out of the city.

When the play opened to the general public, with enough money on hand to keep it running for only a few days, the critics praised it in words of unaccustomed sentimentality and clear purpose. The *World-Telegraph and Sun* reviewer said the public would find the play "absolutely marvelous" and that "Money should be running out of Papp's ears." The *Journal-American* reviewer too wrote a skillfully pitched plea for contributions to the festival. "This seems to me," he suggested, "an excellent opportunity to get the title 'patron of the arts' included in one's biography."

As each week began, Papp was forced to announce that it would be the last, unless more money came in. Each week, all through January and February, he barely managed to keep going.

The largest single gift, of $3,000, came from the New York Foundation, which had given two other donations during the previous ten months. There were other sizable gifts too: $500 from an attorney, $1,000 from the American Academy of Arts and Letters; a personal gift from Harold Cullman who had headed the unsuccessful fund-raising drive the previous fall, and a pledge from the well-known theatrical writer-and-composer team, Richard Rodgers and

Oscar Hammerstein II, to match every $100 gift from other contributors. Rodgers and Hammerstein were also repeating donors to the festival; they had given it $1,000 the year before.

As You Like It survived until the third week in February. By then Papp had abandoned plans to follow it with *Antony and Cleopatra*. He was going to concentrate all his energies on collecting funds for the summer ahead.

In March a "Shapkespeare in Music" concert for the benefit of the festival was held in Carnegie Hall. In April the festival benefited from a "Symphony of the Air." By then, too, Cullman and the actor Ralph Bellamy were completing their plans for a new fund-raising drive.

Like many other friends of the festival, Cullman and Bellamy had long believed that it particularly deserved support from those businesses which profited from tourists, convention delegates and other visitors to the city—such businesses as hotels, restaurants and entertainment enterprises. The owners of those businesses, in their publicity designed to lure people to the city, listed the Shakespeare Festival as one of the town's liveliest attractions. Therefore, Cullman and Bellamy reasoned, they should feel a special responsibility for aiding it, and might be willing to "buy" each of the festival's 2,000 seats in return for seat-back plaques bearing their names as donors.

In the spring of 1958, during a single three-week period, Joseph Papp and his festival group won a total of seven honors. Among them was a special Tony Award from the American Theater Wing, an award to Vaughan for outstanding direction, and an acting award to the already sought-after George C. Scott. (He and his wife, Colleen Dewhurst, who had met during their work with the festival, would remain its loyal friends; they followed Papp's lead when they later founded and helped finance the Theater of Michigan in Detroit—as did the people who eventually founded theaters similar to Papp's in Washington and other cities.)

At about the same time, that spring, Papp was invited to take his group to Philadelphia in June, to open that city's new Playhouse in the Park with a production of *Othello*.

All these events proved harbingers of a good season. Before the end of May, 1958, $15,000 had been raised for the festival—enough to assure a four-week run of *Othello* in New York after its Philadelphia premiere. Still more money was raised with the aid of a new group of supporters, the sportswear manufacturers of the city's large fashion industry. They gave a cocktail party for the festival's benefit, with an admission fee of $25. Before and after that highly successful affair Papp was interviewed by the press and over the air. Interest in what he was trying to do for New York seemed to be spreading in every direction.

That interest did not diminish noticeably when, in June, Papp lost his job at CBS for the same reason that many people in the world of the arts were suffering economically at that period. Called to testify before the then active House Un-American Activities Committee, he refused to answer when asked if he was a Communist, and invoked the Fifth Amendment to protect his silence. Unlike many people who endured similar loss of employment, however, Papp sued and was reinstated in his job after an arbitration ruling.

By July 11, in spite of the fact that Cullman and Bellamy had by no means reached their goal, Papp's costs for a full summer season were at hand. Half the sum had been contributed in amounts of $1 or less. Donations at the performances averaged $300 a night.

Papp followed *Othello* with *Twelfth Night,* chiefly because he could put that play on for only $1,500 a week, by utilizing old costumes and sets. It too was a critical and popular success. The season ended as satisfactorily as it had begun.

Success brought a kind of caution. Papp decided that during the winter he would present only one full play at the Heckscher, *Antony and Cleopatra,* and present it for only one week. He wanted to give the cast that would be assembled for the following summer that much of a chance to work together as a team. During the rest of the winter he meant to present only concert readings of various scenes from the next summer's plays, using the actors that would appear in those productions, but no expensive costumes or sets.

When *Antony and Cleopatra* opened, however, before a paid first-night audience that brought in $2,500, its reception was so enthusiastic that Papp extended the run to three weeks. A review in *Show Business* was typical of the kind of notices he received. "This is an open love letter to Joseph Papp," it began.

As spring approached, a number of civic organizations were planning to put their weight behind a new campaign for obtaining municipal support for the festival. Then, in mid-April, came a totally unexpected blow from a powerful figure who had formerly given the festival his blessing. Robert Moses was commissioner of the city's parks and chief planner of the vast program of public works then changing the face of the metropolitan area. To many he represented the very spirit of municipal progress, although his explosive temperament had led one New Yorker to describe him as sometimes a benign oligarch, sometimes a god of wrath.

Moses now declared that Papp must charge admission to his plays and give the Parks Department part of the fees he collected. If he failed to do so, Moses decreed, Papp's permit to perform in Central Park would be canceled. The Parks Department needed the money, Moses claimed, to pay for restoring the grass "eroded" during the season by the Shakespeare audiences.

Few dared to cross swords with Robert Moses. Papp's reaction to the ruling must have been as startling to the commissioner himself as it was to most New Yorkers. Papp refused to change his policy.

"Do people sitting and watching a play create more of an erosion problem than football, softball, soccer, and similar sports encouraged by the parks at no cost to the players?" he asked publicly.

The resulting controversy made front-page news under such headlines as:

MOSES KICKS UP STORM
ON FEES FOR BARD IN PARK

"A good way to find out how strong an idea has become is to try to stop it," one critic wrote. Moses, he continued, "a man of varied talents, has never been a good judge of public opinion and periodically finds himself playing the role of villain to a large and aroused audience. No one has explained why he turned on the Festival after earlier expressions of approval, but it is obvious that he did not foresee a formidable uprising on behalf of Shakespeare."

Papp's supporters urged Mayor Robert Wagner to intervene. Wagner said he would discuss the matter with Moses as soon as he could "catch up with him." Days went by. Letters of protest against the Moses ruling deluged the mayor's office and filled columns of newsprint. Actors Equity took its stand in favor of Papp. So did youth groups and parent groups. Civic leaders, several elected officials, and the influential Brooks Atkinson declared they backed Papp's stand. A We Want Will Committee was formed. The sober publication of the Citizens Union, moved to verse, published a sonnet titled "Barred Bard" which began

Let us not to the showing of fine plays
Impose impediment. . . .

Before Mayor Wagner could "catch up" with Moses,. Moses was hospitalized with an attack of virus pneumonia. At about the same time Moses mailed to several city officials an unsigned letter which he said he had just received. It was highly derogatory of Papp, who, when he was shown a copy, called it "sickening." He later learned it had been written by an actor who did not get a role he had hoped for with the festival. The letter referred to Papp's "socialist background" and asserted that Papp had refused to answer questions before a Congressional committee about his "Communist background."

Most public officials who received copies of the letter refused to comment on it. An assistant superintendent of schools, an admirer of Papp's productions for the city's students, did say tartly, "So far as I know, Shakespeare was never a Communist. I suppose," he added, "if he were alive today, someone might call him one." The mayor, prodded for his reaction, said he had not seen the letter but that "on the principle of it . . . I have never used the practice of unsigned letters. I do not approve the technique."

Still the mayor did not rescind Moses' decision. If he did so, he said, he would have to get another parks commissioner, and he did not want to lose the valuable Mr. Moses.

Robert Wagner then also became the object of public scorn. A cartoon showed him standing over the slain figure of Shakespeare, above the caption "Et tu, Bob?"

Papp, ignoring the advice of friends who urged him not to tangle with the formidable Moses, did exactly what he would have done if his antagonist had been of lesser stature: He petitioned the state's Supreme Court to compel Moses to let the festival continue on a free basis. On June 2 the court, openly sympathetic to Papp, but reluctant to interfere with the decision of any municipal commissioner, dismissed the petition. Moses, the judges said, had "full discretion" on the theatrical performances that might be staged in the park.

The city of Newark, across the Hudson River in New Jersey, promptly let it be known that Papp's festival would be welcomed there. Papp refused to take that way out of his dilemma. Instead, again against the advice of friends, he took the unusual step of asking the appellate division of the courts to hear an appeal from the Supreme Court's dismissal of his case.

Papp knew the judges were unlikely to grant his request. He knew that even if they agreed to do so, their crowded calendar would probably not permit them to hold a hearing before several months had passed.

But Papp and his volunteer lawyer were suddenly ordered to appear before the appellate division. On June 17—little more than two weeks after Papp's earlier suit had been dismissed—the five judges unanimously concurred in the statement that Moses had been "clearly arbitrary, capricious and unreasonable" in not permitting Papp to stage his plays for nonpaying audiences.

The unexpected decision was reported in gleeful headlines. Papp was hailed as a hero who had bearded the lion in his den.

The triumph was clouded briefly by the judges' additional statement that Moses had the right to set some conditions for a permit, and by Moses's immediate announcement that he would grant a permit only if "funds in the minimum of $20,000" were provided to put the theater area of the park "in condition for safe, controllable and reasonably satisfactory temporary use."

Papp said he could not possibly raise such a sum in time to make use of a permit that summer. While friends pleaded with the city's Board of Estimate to give him the money—even Moses himself unexpectedly asked the board to provide it—the $20,000 was contributed by two private sources, the E. L. Bernays Foundation and the L. K. Anspacher Trust. Actors who had been waiting for weeks for the outcome of the crisis went into immediate rehearsal. *Julius Caesar* opened in Central Park in the first week of August.

It was a gala occasion. One critic wrote that every member of the audience clearly regarded his seat as a symbol of "the victory of vox populi."

New Yorkers who felt they had helped save the

festival by their protests flocked to the park theater in greater numbers than ever during the following weeks. They were united not only by their love of the starlit plays but also in the knowledge of having aided in the happy outcome of the city's newest folk tale: the story of Papp and Shakespeare versus Moses and his "grass erosion." The *New Yorker* magazine's satirical account of the struggle was popular reading among the nightly theatergoers.

"I am sure we shall all sleep easier these summer nights for knowing that the Commissioner is on the *qui vive* against the perils of erosion in the heart of our city," the *New Yorker* author John Sack had written. He told his readers that Moses, aware that erosion could produce such tragedies as a Grand Canyon, was probably also aware of the "Bard's own warnings against soil erosion." And he asked the public's sympathy for a Moses who he suggested might some night "stand in the shadows behind an audience during, say, the first act of a performance of 'Richard II,' his ear already attuned to the rough scrapings of two thousand pairs of feet upon his precious grass, and hear a talented actor cry out, 'Sweet soil, adieu!' "

Before the end of August Moses was asking the City Planning Commission to appropriate $250,000 to build a permanent outdoor theater in Central Park where Papp's plays could be produced in future summers. A new Citizens Committee, formed to work for the permanent support of the festival, lauded the plan. Helen Hayes and Marilyn Monroe were two of the many well-known theatrical figures who appeared before the commission to urge the appropriation. In December of that same year, 1959, the city allocated funds for the theater, with the understanding that Papp would provide enough money to produce ten-week seasons during each of the next two summers.

"We'll be flat broke when we finish here," Papp had said before the end of the 1959 summer season, "flat broke. Every year we start again from the bottom."

But by now he was used to that. Raising money had become a way of life. Besides, as one critic said, "He has steady nerves and is capable of opening a play when he has no funds beyond the first night."

In actual fact Papp was never again to be in quite such serious straits. He could not always put on the full season he had hoped for, but by 1960 he had a budget large enough to include a salary for himself. He was thus able to give up his television job and for the first time devote himself exclusively to the mounting demands of his rapidly expanding festival. He even managed to fit some teaching into his busy schedule, and to appear as an occasional guest director with other outstanding companies.

One of his first projects in 1960 was a festival subscription program: He invited people who had previously written in for free tickets to become festival patrons at $7.50 each, in return for which they would be guests at special previews of all productions. The response was large and immediate. Thousands of New

Yorkers proved willing to contribute that sum to the festival, so that thousands of others could see the plays without cost.

The next year Papp was touring schools with *Henry V* on a budget of $82,000, of which 60 percent had been contributed by the Board of Education.

In the meantime George T. Delacorte, a New York City publisher, had added $150,000 to the city's appropriation for a festival theater and the structure was being completed. Papp moved his company into its new home, known as the Delacorte Theater, in 1962. Looking at the tiers of seats rising in an arc about the stage, Papp remarked that the theater had been built out of "twenty-five hundred planks and a passion." He himself directed *The Merchant of Venice,* with George S. Scott as Shylock, for the Delacorte's premiere.

"This festival is a memorial to his persistence and his belief in Shakespeare," Mayor Wagner said of Papp at the opening night's ceremonies.

Later that season CBS-TV televised the play, as it was to do with other plays in subsequent years.

Two years later Delacorte gave the festival a new $35,000 mobile stage designed by Ming Cho Lee. The 40-foot stage trailer provided a stage 20 feet wide and 14 feet deep. The new equipment also included a control truck, a generator, two dressing-room trailers, and vehicles for transporting the cast and seats for the audience.

A grant of $170,000 from the city permitted Papp

to put the new stage immediately to work. That same summer of 1964 he used it to present *A Midsummer Night's Dream* in thirty-nine city parks and playgrounds, and then toured the city's Spanish-speaking neighborhoods with a Spanish-language production of two plays by Federico Garcia Lorca.

Papp celebrated the four hundredth anniversary of Shakespeare's birth that year with special productions of *Othello* and *Hamlet,* but the Lorca plays were not the only non-Shakespearean works he put on. "I'm no crazy Bardophile," he had often told people who believed he wanted to do nothing but Shakespeare. Now he was proving it by staging Sophocles's *Electra* during the Shakespeare Anniversary Year. In future years, though Shakespeare would remain a major source of his productions, Papp would frequently experiment with other plays, old and new.

Having achieved a permanent summer theater, Papp applied his energies to acquiring a year-round home for his festival. While he built up a fund toward its purchase, he sought the ideal site. He found what he wanted in a part of New York already the home of several experimental theaters, and close to the neighborhood where he had first put on free Shakespeare performances in a church basement ten years earlier. It was a dignified 115-year-old red brick and sandstone building which had been constructed as the Astor Library, but allowed to fall into such disrepair that it was slated for demolition. A real estate operator had made a down payment of $15,000 against its selling price of $575,000, with the intent of selling his interest at a profit to a contractor who would raze it and replace it with a new structure.

Papp first managed to get the old library declared a city landmark, so that it could not be destroyed without considerable legal red tape. Then he approached the real estate operator and offered to buy the man's interest in the building for the $15,000 he had paid for it. The real estate man's discouraging answer was that he was in business to make money. He wanted $35,000.

"Sure you want to make money," Papp told him. "But why make it on us?

" 'Listen,' I told him," he remembered later, " 'why don't you make a contribution to your city? Be a fine citizen. Make your profits somewhere else. Help us establish the kind of theater we think New York needs. You'll be a benefactor to your fellowman. And you can get a tax allowance for your contribution besides.' "

Like many other objects of Papp's persuasiveness, the man finally agreed. Papp got his building. With Ming Cho Lee, principal stage designer for the festival, and architect Giorgio Cavaglieri, he set to work immediately to plan remodeling the old library into the New York Shakespeare Festival Public Theater.

Within it, he announced, he would eventually have three theaters and ample space for rehearsal halls, workshop classrooms and offices.

At the same time Papp was trying to raise enough

money to complete the first of those three theaters he dreamed of—an intimate arena-stage theater with only 299 seats, the maximum seating allowed to theaters granted special concessions by actors' and technicians' unions. Papp employed one fund-raising technique that had been tried on his festival's behalf earlier.

"I'm going on a chair campaign," he told the press. "One thousand dollars a chair. If I sell them all, that's two hundred ninty-nine thousand dollars." He "sold" the dressing rooms too, one pair of them to Mr. and Mrs. Richard Burton.

With the aid of a $125,000 grant from the National Council on the Arts he raised the $1,000,000 he needed to open that small theater, named the Florence Sutro Anspacher Theater for its chief benefactor. He was launching a drive for another $2,000,000, to complete the center, when he opened his first season in the building in the fall of 1967.

The new little theater drew admiring notices. One critic said its high vaulted ceiling—it had been constructed in what had once been the main reading room of the library—and its steeply banked red-velvet seats evoked a "great feeling of occasion and opulence."

The performance was just as enthusiastically received, although many were surprised at Papp's choice of a play. Under the direction of Gerald Freedman, who had been principal director for the company since 1960, he presented the rock-pop musical *Hair,* by two young lyricists, Gerome Ragni and James Rado, and the young composer Galt MacDermot. *Newsweek's* reviewer said it "ignites the key images and issues of the lost-and-found generation—youth vs. age, sex, love, the draft, race, drugs, Vietnam —into a vivid uproar that has more wit, feeling and musicality than anything since 'West Side Story.' "

Other new experimental plays followed. Papp wanted to appeal to young people, including those whose first theatrical experience might have been at one of his free neighborhood performances, by giving them plays directly related to their own time and their own lives. He charged admission, but at such a low figure that he hoped it would not keep away even the least affluent. He also exhibited the work of young artists in the lobby. And he invited all comers to write their comments on life, love, war and the arts on the white walls of a small room opening off the lobby. Even the black crayons were provided. He could not prevent the middle-aged from filling many of the seats of his new theater, but they were not the people to whom he most wished to appeal.

As the winter wore on, Papp was busy as always preparing for his next summer season. Some of his productions would be classical Shakespeare. He planned to produce both Part I and Part II of *Henry IV,* and to put on *Romeo and Juliet* again, this time with young Martin Sheen who had just repeated for Hollywood a starring role he had played on Broadway. Sheen could have commanded a far larger salary elsewhere, but he chose to work with Papp because, he said, "He's a marvelous man, the most joyful man in the theater

. . . . His is the only theater I care about in the country. It's the only one that has anything to give."

For that same summer Papp was also planning to present his highly controversial version of Hamlet, to be presented throughout the city's parks on his mobile stage. (The performances were scheduled to run only through July for the usual reason: lack of funds to run longer.) His Hamlet was a hipster and his Ophelia a teeny-bopper. On the same mobile stage, during the afternoon, he would also present *Take One Step,* a new children's musical based on the old Pied Piper story.

Full-page newspaper ads, paid for by a New York department store, hailed the opening of that summer season. "All New York's a stage as the Mobile Theater rolls again," the ads announced, listing the time and place of every scheduled performance. "Will would have loved it!" the ads declared.

New Yorkers were not surprised to see such expensive newspaper space, paid for by a business enterprise, devoted to the Shakespeare Festival. They found it perfectly natural, by then, that even the city's department stores should get into the act of promoting the city's own theater.

"It was obvious, when Joseph Papp was starting his New York Shakespeare Festival, that Mr. Papp was out of his mind," someone had written a few years earlier. Even now there are those who think he must be insane to refuse the lucrative posts regularly offered to him, in favor of spending his life producing and directing, teaching and writing, and everlastingly grubbing for the funds necessary to maintain his constantly more ambitious theatrical program.

But for Papp there are rewards enough in the love and devotion of actors and audiences no longer dispossessed. And one critic undoubtedly spoke for hundreds of thousands of his admirers when he quoted a Moss Hart line which, the critic said, always evoked for him Papp and his company: "Mad, sire? Yes, sire, they are mad, but observe how they do light up the sky!"

About the Authors

Beryl Williams was born in Columbus, Ohio; Samuel Epstein in Boston, Massachusetts. They studied at Rutgers University in New Jersey, were married and began their long and successful collaboration.

As a free-lance writing team, Beryl and Sam Epstein are the authors of more than 125 books. The titles range over a wide variety of subjects, requiring extensive research. *The Andrews Raid,* the story of a daring hijack of a Confederate locomotive, was published by Coward-McCann in 1956.

At present, the Epsteins make their home in Southold, New York.